FOOD THROUGH THE AGES

FOOD THROUGH THE AGES

From Stuffed Dormice to Pineapple Hedgehogs

by Anna Selby

First published in Great Britain in 2008 by
REMEMBER WHEN
an imprint of
Pen & Sword Books Ltd
47 Church Street
Barnsley
South Yorkshire
S70 2AS

ISBN 978 1 84468 027 6

A CIP catalogue record for this book is
available from the British Library

Picture Editor: David L Hemingway
Picture Researcher: Fiona Shoop

Printed and bound in Singapore
By Kyodo Printing Co (Singapore) Pte Ltd

Pen & Sword Books Ltd incorporates the imprints of
Pen & Sword Aviation, Pen & Sword Maritime, Pen & Sword Military,
Wharncliffe Local History, Pen & Sword Select, Pen & Sword Military Classics,
Leo Cooper, Remember When, Seaforth Publishing and Frontline Publishing

For a complete list of Pen & Sword titles please contact
PEN & SWORD BOOKS LIMITED
47 Church Street, Barnsley, South Yorkshire, S70 2AS, England
E-mail: enquiries@pen-and-sword.co.uk
Website: www.pen-and-sword.co.uk

Contents

Introduction

'Tell me what you eat, and I shall tell you what you are.'
Jean Anthelme Brillat-Savarin (1755–1826)

THE STORY of food is the story of humankind. From the first hunter-gatherers who roamed across continents in search of prey, to the farmers who worked the land they lived on, what people ate and how they came by it defined their entire existence. Food was the ultimate necessity while at the same time being deeply symbolic. In the earliest societies, the slaughter of an animal was a ritual, with the first portion allotted to the gods before mere men could taste it. After farming was established, bread became the main staple, synonymous with food in general, and even enshrined in the Lord's Prayer. Breaking bread was always a symbolic act – of the obligation of the host to welcome his guest, of sharing, of friendship itself. The very word 'companion' comes from the Latin meaning 'one with whom you share bread'.

Food, though, is not only about the assuagement of hunger, it relates also to the palate. 'Taste' is a word whose origins clearly lie with food but whose meaning reaches far beyond it, embracing everything from an appreciation of fine paintings to our personal behaviour. In fact, much of that behaviour relates directly to food. From the ancient Greeks onwards, food and how we prepared and ate it revealed how civilised we were. The Greeks themselves preferred to eat while lying on couches, watering their wine to enhance their after dinner discussion, or symposium – evidence that there have always been rules and rituals surrounding the table. Even in the Middle Ages – mostly imagined as a time when rude knights threw bones over their shoulders to the dogs on the floor – there was a strict etiquette about where you sat, what you ate and the order in which you were served. And as the centuries went on the etiquette of dining became more and more important. 'Good taste' – our degree of civilisation – could be gauged by how we passed the vegetables or how we ate our peas.

Food is also a profoundly social event; there is still some opprobrium or at least something inherently sad about dinner for one. We invite friends for dinner, and all major religious and family events – Christmas, weddings, even funerals – are accompanied by feasts. Feasting traditionally meant meat. We now eat more meat than our ancestors could dream of, but for millennia there were days, weeks and even months when there would be no meat on the table for reasons both of agricultural necessity and religious observance. In the seasons and festivals when animals were slaughtered, the rich would hold extravagant banquets, accompanied by all kinds of lavish entertainment – and even the poor would eat more than usual.

When we eat has changed remarkably over the centuries, too. Dinner was always the main meal, but it has moved back around eight hours since the Middle Ages. Originally it was the first meal of the day (at least for the nobility who rose later; the servants might have had a snatched break-fast on rising) taken at around eleven o'clock in the morning. By Jane Austen's time it generally took place at three in the afternoon but just a century later, dinner shifted back to the evening and a new meal, lunch or luncheon took its place in the middle of the day. Dinner in the evening was a substantial meal, but a smaller meal was also sometimes taken and this was known as supper. There is still some confusion over these terms and in different parts of England meals are given the same names to mean different things. In the north, for instance, dinner is still the main midday meal and the evening meal which can be quite substantial is nevertheless known as tea. In the south, however, dinner or supper is the evening meal, and tea is an occasional meal that is taken around four o'clock and comprises sandwiches, scones – and a pot of tea.

This book traces the history of food from the earliest recorded civilisations to the present day. From the ancient Egyptian labourer to the Edwardian shooting party, from Medieval banquets to the rationing of the Second World War, what people ate and into how they ate it gives an extraordinary insight both into the lives of our ancestors and as to how our own contemporary approach to food has evolved.

Chapter 1

The Ancient World

L ET'S go right back to the beginning – in so far as we know it. The staples of the ancient Egyptian diet were bread and beer – mortuary offerings often bear the inscription 'bread, beer and all good things'. And, for the poor, there was probably not much more than that, just some vegetables and fish from the Nile, either dried, boiled, fried or roasted, or occasional game in the shape of quails, ducks and cranes. The rich, on the other hand, shunned fish and ate game in the form of various kinds of antelope and the

Pomegranates, enjoyed since Ancient times, were believed to give wisdom.

meat from domesticated animals, such as beef, pork, goose, mutton and duck instead, though even the rich probably didn't eat them as often as we do today – they were too expensive a commodity to raise in such an arid land. The rich also drank wine besides the ubiquitous beer.

As well as having a greater choice in meat, the diet for the rich was a surprisingly varied and sophisticated one. It featured olive oil and figs and food was flavoured with herbs and spices such as cumin, coriander and cinnamon, thyme, dill and fennel. Under the warm Egyptian sun, fruit and vegetables were grown and eaten widely, especially onions, garlic and green vegetables. They were generally recognised in ancient Egypt as health giving foods (as, of course, has been established scientifically today) though through later millennia they were to be eschewed by all but the poorest. Local grapes, watermelon, figs, pomegranates and dates were eaten by rich and poor alike, while olives, peaches and cherries were imported. One of the most widely used foods was honey, and not just as a sweetener. It was highly regarded for its medicinal properties (honey being a powerful antiseptic) and beeswax was used as an essential part of the process of mummification.

Everyone, both rich and poor,

Nuts provided a staple part of the diet in Ancient civilisation.

Corn Dollies

The corn god in ancient Egypt and Babylon was Tammuz, the son of Ishtar, mother of the universe. At the end of every harvest, special refuges for him were constructed out of the last sheaves plaited into fans or cages and these were the very first corn idols or dollies that were to proliferate throughout every wheat-growing country for millennia. In the Balkans, the fan shape of the original Egyptian dolly persisted, known as the Montenegrin Fan. In England, corn dollies were to appear in many guises. There were Shropshire Mares, Derbyshire Crowns, Kern Babbies and Ivy Girls – all daughters of their Egyptian mother, Ishtar.

ate bread every day and the ancient Egyptians produced a prodigious amount of grain along the banks of the Nile. It was the river's annual flooding that gave Egypt its fertile soil and made it one of the earliest civilisations with a highly developed form of agriculture. Besides bread, the grain harvest was used to make pastries and cakes, flavoured with honey, fruits, sesame and nuts. Flat bread was sometimes baked with eggs poured into hollows and, of course, some of the cereal went to make the barley beer. The production of the flour was, literally, a daily grind. The process meant pounding, grinding and milling, all of which

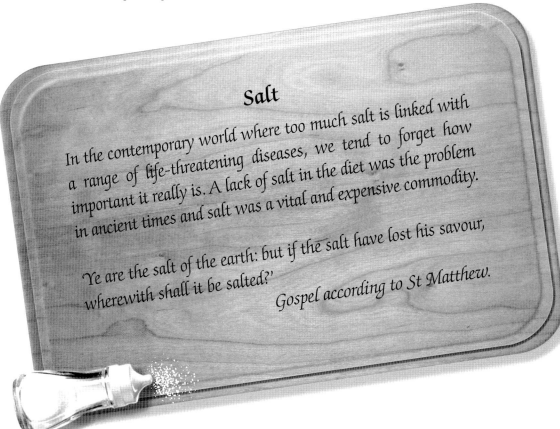

Salt

In the contemporary world where too much salt is linked with a range of life-threatening diseases, we tend to forget how important it really is. A lack of salt in the diet was the problem in ancient times and salt was a vital and expensive commodity.

Ye are the salt of the earth: but if the salt have lost his savour, wherewith shall it be salted?'

Gospel according to St Matthew.

were done by hand while the cook sat on the ground out of doors, where a good many unwanted ingredients inevitably found their way into the flour.

Egyptian cooking took place out of doors, too, over open wood fires or in clay ovens, reducing the risk of fire. And, although the cooking methods were basic, ancient tombs show plenty of fine storage jars and bowls. Rich Egyptians ate off bronze, silver and even gold, while the poor had to make do with clay.

An Egyptian Dish

Hummus

This is a simple dish that is still popular today throughout the Middle East. It can be used as a dip for vegetables or pitta bread or as a side dish with salads and falafels

225g / 8oz chick peas

2 tbsp white wine vinegar

3 cloves of garlic, crushed

5 tbsp olive oil

1 tsp salt

Juice of 1 lemon

Soak the chick peas overnight, bring to the boil in fresh water, boil fast for 10 minutes, then simmer for a further 40 minutes. Drain and mash (or use a food processor) with the other ingredients.

ANCIENT HOSPITALITY

Hospitality was a concept central to the Ancient World. In Biblical times, one of the best known stories from the life of Jesus tells of when he was welcomed into a house as an honoured guest, where his feet were washed and anointed with expensive oils. In Greece there was a sacred duty to take care of the stranger, who brought news of wars and marriages, festivities and disasters, in a time when other forms of communication were limited to say the least. Food, and with it feasting, was one of the principal ways in which to welcome, to form a bond and cement alliances. For all these reasons, guests were honoured: they were served first and given the choicest foods.

On the other hand, this bond could be abused, too. Penelope, the wife of Odysseus, was obliged to host her numerous unprepossessing suitors for the

many years of her husband's absence while they eroded her herds and cellars. The ultimate crime in ancient Greece was the murder of a guest – hence the power of the epic story of the returning Agamemnon. Home from the Trojan War, he is murdered by his wife Clytemnestra and her lover Aegisthus (who also happened to be Agamemnon's own cousin) at the banquet they hold in his honour. And, while Greeks were generally rather more well-behaved than this at the table, they could, like Hooray Henry, indulge in food fights. There was one game in particular that involved the swinging of a wine cup with the aim that its contents ended up on a bronze dish. No doubt they frequently missed.

The Symposium

Although the ancient Greeks usually sat to eat as we do, at formal all-male dinners they tended to lie down on couches and this is how we mostly picture them. At these dinners, rather than having a communal table, everyone had a small individual table of his own. The tables would appear with the food already on them, and serve as a plate, too. They could be wiped down and more food could be placed on them, or new tables would bring in new courses. It is thought that the Greeks adopted the idea of lying on couches during meals after having observed Assyrians and Phoenicians in this pose.

The couch itself was regarded as a symbol of prestige and so it was only the upper classes and, of them, only men who were permitted to use it. Women were never allowed to join them on the couches – unless they were the prostitutes or dancing girls brought in as part of the entertainment. Any other women who on rare occasions might attend would be seated – regarded as a far inferior position to lying on the couch. The dining couch could be quite a distance from the ground and require a footstool to mount it. The diner then had to lie on his left elbow and eat using his right hand. At the end of dinner, guests would wipe their hands on bread and throw it to the dogs, along with any leftovers or bones. This practice would continue well into the Middle Ages.

One school of thought believes that the same system was current in biblical times. The Last Supper would have taken place reclining on couches and not in the manner everyone knows from Leonardo da Vinci's famous painting. The apostle John is seen in da Vinci's picture leaning rather awkwardly on Christ's shoulder, but in the original Greek he is described as 'leaning back on his master's chest', as he would have done during a reclining conversation.

Later, came the drinking part of the evening and this was quite separate from the dinner. To mark the turning point, after the dishes were cleared, the guests would perfume themselves and light incense in the room, thereby changing the ambience. The paraphernalia of drinking replaced that of eating. There were ladles, pitchers, cups, a great bowl (known as a krater) for mixing water and wine and even pitchers of snow to cool the wine. A libation, or offering to the gods (often to Dionysus, god of wine), of the first of the wine was made before the drinking began among the men. The wine was never drunk 'neat' but diluted so that there was slightly more water than wine in the cup, enabling the enlightened conversation of the symposium to take place. And such talks! They were to become the basis of the *Symposiums* of Plato and Plutarch. The wine fuelled the flow of conversation and, incidentally, drinking your wine without water was almost a definition of barbarism, believed to lead in all probability to madness and death.

The Mediterranean triad

For the first part of their history, at least, the Greeks were modest in their appetite for food, regarding Epicureanism as something that undermined the strength of nations – as witnessed by Alexander the Great when he conquered the immensely powerful but morally decadent Persian Empire, grown corpulent on sweetmeats. The life of the animal given up so that people could eat was regarded with respect. Every time an animal was slaughtered, particular parts of it – the bones and the fat – would be set aside as an offering to the gods, while the meat was reserved for human consumption. Over time, though, the Greeks became less devout and food and religion went their separate ways. The pleasures of the table became an end in themselves and wealthy men would employ their own accomplished cooks and leave the preparation of it to them. Nevertheless, for the most part, the Greeks preferred simple food and, when not at grand dinners, they had a diet that was based on what became known as the 'Mediterranean triad': wheat, olive oil and wine. They had three meals a day more or less at the same times as we do. Bread, usually flat bread, was the staple and was often flavoured with cheese or honey. It could be made of wheat or barley and was dipped in wine or olive oil for breakfast.

Pumpkin Pie

Although it sounds like the ultimate American dessert, pumpkin pie was popular among the ancient Greeks, orange pumpkins being common in Thrace (an ancient country lying west of the Black Sea and north of the Aegean). The same dish could be made with courgettes – both are savoury rather than sweet.

Serves 6
1 large pumpkin or 6 courgettes
4 tbsp olive oil
4 eggs divided into white and yolks
4 tbsp plain flour
300g / 10^{1}/$_{2}$oz feta cheese
Salt and freshly ground pepper, to taste

Grate the pumpkin, sprinkle with salt and leave for 2–3 hours. Sauté the pumpkin in the oil. Cool and add the egg yolks and flour. Stir in the cheese and seasoning. Pour into a large (25cm / 10in) greased and floured baking pan. Bake at 200°C / 400°F / gas mark 6 for 30 minutes.

Pumpkin pie was a classic dish enjoyed by the Ancient Greeks.

Other mainstays included vegetables, such as cabbage, onion and beans, often turned into soup, and also salads, such as rocket, lettuce, cucumbers and cress. Fruits – figs, oranges, quinces and pomegranates – formed the main dessert, served with nuts. The Greeks also regularly used lentils and beans, eggs, honey and cheese in cooking, and their flavourings included dill, mint, pepper, oregano, saffron and thyme.

The wealthier you were, the more meat you were likely to eat. It came from goats, pigs, poultry and sheep, but so valuable were farmed animals generally that when one was slaughtered, every last bit of it was used. If you lived close to the sea (a fifth of Greece comprises islands) you would eat more fish and

Greek Mullet

Mullet is a favourite Mediterranean fish. Here it is simply stuffed with herbs and grilled. Serves 6

> 6 small red mullets
> 3 tbsp olive oil
> 2 handfuls of herbs such as thyme, mint and dill
> Salt and freshly milled pepper

Have the fish cleaned by the fishmonger. Mix the oil, herbs and seasoning and use to stuff the fish, smearing any leftover mixture over the top of the fish. Grill for 5 minutes on each side.

Tributes to Aphrodite

The Greeks were firm believers in the powers of aphrodisiacs (the name is taken from the Greek goddess of love and beauty, Aphrodite). Favourite foods for increased sexual prowess and stamina included artichokes and bean soup – a pretty lethal combination. Perhaps the most renowned aphrodisiacs, however, were edible bulbs, notably the *museari comosum*, the grape hyacinth, which would be boiled, then marinated in vinegar and finally served drizzled with olive oil.

shellfish. Local specialities varied, too. The Mycenaeans liked beef and kid, while Spartans ate mostly pork and a black gruel for which they were famed. In addition, there were numerous special diets for everyone from vegetarians to training athletes.

Chapter 2

The Romans

NERO was famous not only for his musicianship at inappropriate moments, he held banquets renowned for their lavishness, too. The food would be exotic and extravagant and his guests were treated to the most theatrical of experiences. Beneath the domed ceiling of his banqueting hall, which reflected the heavens with the stars and planets moving as they would in the sky, they were showered during their feasting with flowers and sprinkled with perfumed oils.

This was just one rather extreme end of the Roman economic spectrum, however, and at a time when the imperial family's excesses were at their height. Other periods and other classes lived very differently. The poor ate frugally, their diet consisting mostly of bread, and pea or bean broth, olive oil and a little fish. If they were peasants wealthy enough to own chickens or a cow, they might have milk, cheese or eggs. All classes, though, relied above all on grains – principally barley, wheat and millet – as their staple food. Much of the grain came from Egypt, often described as the 'bread basket' of the Roman Empire and it was used in a wide variety of ways. It could be ground into flour for the round, flat, unleavened bread that was common at the time and can still be seen in Greece, Turkey and the Middle East today. Among the poor, the grain could also be made into a gruel, called *puls*. Sweet cakes and pastries, flavoured with honey, were popular, too.

The moderately rich enjoyed a varied diet with plenty of fruit, such as figs and grapes; vegetables, including leeks, asparagus, onion, garlic, radishes, courgettes and marrows, cabbage and lettuce; fish and shellfish; and the most expensive ingredient, meat, most commonly lamb or goat. Olives were

Fresh fish was plentiful only for those living near the sea or rivers. The lack of suitable methods of preservation meant people inland had to rely on smoked, dried or salted fish.

ubiquitous and olive oil was used in many dishes. Cheese – fresh, smoked, local or imported – and eggs were both popular. Honey was the only widely available sweetener and used in all kinds of cooked dishes, in cakes and simply as a delicious sop for bread. As a result, bee-keeping was an important Roman industry.

Wherever they went, the Romans built roads, cities and baths and took their foods and preferred tastes with them. They brought wine, herbs and spices to all corners of the empire and introduced many new foods. Though often assumed to be a native, it was the Romans, for instance, who introduced the apple to Britain. The crab apple *was* native to these islands, but having a sour taste it was not to be compared with the fruit produced in the Roman orchards.

The daily routine of the Romans was similar to the one we have today, though many centuries passed in between their society and ours when mealtimes were quite different. Breakfast, or *ientaculum*, was similar to that of the ancient Greeks with some bread dipped in watered-down wine and perhaps some honey, olives or dates. Lunch, or *prandium*, was a light meal again based around bread, with any of the breakfast dishes, together with some cheese and fruit. The main meal was dinner, or *cena*, and this took place in the late afternoon or evening. For the poor it was usually more bread, vegetables and olive oil; but for the rich, even when they were not entertaining or holding a banquet, it would consist of three courses and plenty of wine.

The first course (*gustatio* or *promulsis*) consisted of such hors-d'œuvres as egg dishes, salads that might have both raw and cooked vegetables and, depending on the extravagance of the occasion, snails, oysters and baked dormice. The second course (*lena* or *prima mensa*, literally 'first table') was much the same as our own main course, in that meat or fish was the principal ingredient. This might be suckling pig, peacock, pheasant or goose, served in rich sauces with various side dishes. The last course was the *secunda mensa*, literally 'second table' and this alluded to the fact that, for formal dining, the entire table would be removed and replaced with a new one offering fruits, nuts and sweetmeats, such as honey cakes. While watered wine would have been served throughout, it was for after the end of the meal, when the food had been cleared away, that the Romans reserved their finest wines. And guests could expect entertainment too in the form of music or poetry, clowns or jugglers, during and after their dinner.

THE ROMAN KITCHEN

The Romans had a circular domed wood-burning oven for baking bread and pastries, and these were often produced commercially, although baking could also be done at home. There were even portable ovens – presumably of great use as the Romans pressed ever further the boundaries of their empire. In the domestic kitchen, most food would be cooked over an open fire on a raised hearth (about table height) in a cauldron supported on a tripod. Larger cauldrons could be suspended by chains over open fires on the ground and the biggest animals would be cooked on a turning spit over an open fire, too. The food itself was mostly either boiled, or fried in olive oil, and some foods would be wood smoked (such as fish and cheese). As well as the cauldron, there were bronze frying pans (*fretale*) and iron trays for roasting and frying. Shallow pans (*patellae*) and earthenware dishes (*patinae*) brought food to the table. A discus, a large circular platter made of bronze, silver or pewter, carried the food to the table for a formal dinner.

Much food would be locally produced, but wealthy Romans had a great love of the exotic. Unfortunately, they had few means of preserving meat or transporting it quickly so that it would still be edible at the end of the journey. Accordingly, animals or fish that were intended for the table would often be taken to their final destination live, and killed there. And, for a truly exotic dish, the very wealthy might indulge in some fresh meat from the games at the Coliseum – lion or giraffe, perhaps.

Most of what is known about Roman eating habits comes from paintings as the only known cookbook – long attributed to Marcus Gavius Apicius though this is by no means certain – is *De Re Coquinara* (On the subject of cooking). There is also archaeological evidence in the form of dishes and cooking materials. From these various sources it is known that the poor ate off coarse pottery dishes, while the rich preferred fine china, glass and precious metals,

The Roman Focus

The Latin for a hearth is *focus*. And that was exactly what it was – the centre of the home where food was cooked and the family gathered for warmth.

from pewter to gold. Knives with iron blades and bronze or wooden handles were used for cutting, but the food itself was generally eaten with the fingers – there was nothing equivalent to a fork. There were spoons, though, for liquids, and special implements for extracting the snails and shellfish the Romans loved from their shells. Many Romans, especially poor ones, ate sitting at a table as we would today. However, for wealthy diners and at grand banquets it became the fashion to lie down on couches – just as the Greeks had.

The images we know so well of wealthy Romans lolling around on their elbows while slaves bring them roasted larks' tongues gives a very one-sided impression of the approach to food that most Romans had. The Emperor Augustus, for instance, was known for his preference for simpler, peasant-style foods rather than highly flavoured delicacies. And meals were not necessarily long drawn-out affairs enjoyed at your own or someone else's home. There were literally thousands of food shops and taverns, *thermopolia*, in Rome where you could buy mulled wine and snacks such as sausages, bread and cheese. They were used by people who had no cooking facilities of their own, by those who preferred eating out and by a range of such dubious characters that at one stage the Emperor Claudius had all the *thermopoloia* closed down. According to archaeologist Penelope Allison of the University of Leicester, even when the Romans were at home, they were not necessarily gathered together around the *focus* (hearth). After she excavated a neighbourhood of Pompeii, a picture emerged of solitary eating, not dissimilar to modern-day 'grazing', with plates scattered through various rooms, often in bedrooms, a lack of tableware and an absence of a room set aside for dining.

The Romans in Britain

Excavations of Roman remains in Britain have shown that, for the wealthy at least, life was pleasant enough. A typical country villa would have a home farm and, with it, a regular supply of grains and domestic animals for meat, milk, eggs and cheese. Fresh bread was baked daily and there was an abundance of fruit in season including apples, pears, cherries and plums. There were plenty of fish and game to be caught and bees would be kept for honey. Wine was imported from Italy, Spain or France and drunk watered down. The Romans did, though, eventually establish vines in southern Britain.

Roman Sauces

The Romans liked their food highly flavoured. The main flavourings were sweet, salty and sour but they could often be mixed together in the same recipe, for instance, fruit, honey and vinegar would make a sweet-sour sauce for meat. The sauces and flavourings from the capital were to travel with the conquerors throughout their empire and became the basis of recipes all over Europe that were to last well into the Medieval era and even beyond. The herbs and, particularly, spices that the Romans enjoyed were to become highly sought after and extremely expensive. After the end of the empire this made them increasingly difficult to obtain. This longing for the spices that had been around since the Romans introduced them was eventually to drive the opening up of new sea routes and the discoveries of new worlds many centuries later.

- Liquamen was a very strong fish stock and probably the most popular single sauce of the times. It could be made at home through a long process of fermentation of fish and salt in a sealed jar. The resulting sauce would be strained through cloth and used as a cooking sauce for a wide range of dishes, or as a dip for bread. It was so popular that there were many liquamen factories throughout the empire and there is nothing quite like it today – the closest would perhaps be to make a strong fish stock using anchovies, though in contemporary adaptations of Roman recipes, usually simple salt is recommended as the alternative

- Defritum was a sweet, thick syrup made from boiling down mashed figs in water

- Passum was a very sweet sauce made by boiling grape juice and honey

- Popular herbs used in cooking included silphium (similar to garlic), levisticum (similar to celery), fennel, bay leaf, parsley, dill and mint

- Spices were used in great quantities in cooking and included ginger, saffron, cinnamon, cumin and cardamom. • The value of pepper was very high and widely recognised. At the final demise of Rome in the Fifth century, the barbarians at the gates demanded not just land and military titles but 3,000 pounds of pepper

Saffron was one of the most expensive spices but only a tiny amount was needed to infuse a dish with colour as well as flavour.

ROMAN COOKBOOK

Most of the recipes we have from the days of ancient Rome have come to us through the previously mentioned 'De Re Coquinaria', attributed to Marcus Gavius Apicius. Given that many of the ingredients, particularly the sauces and some of the other flavourings, are no longer readily available, the following recipes are contemporary adaptations.

Herb Salad

The cheese in the original recipe would have been salty – use extra salt if you are using cheese without such a strong flavour

> A handful each of fresh mint, coriander and parsley
> 200g / 7oz strongly flavoured cheese
> 2 tsp olive oil
> 1 tsp vinegar
> Black pepper

Very finely chop the herbs, grate the cheese and mix together. Mix together the remaining three ingredients and pour over the salad.

Watering the Wine

Just as the Greeks had, the Romans watered down their wine – unwatered wine was still considered barbaric. Wine was drunk with every meal and by every class of society. Often it was served spiced and warm, like today's mulled wine.

There are few European wine-growing areas that did not once form part of the Roman Empire, and the importance of wine was not simply that it was the most popular drink, it had religious significance, too. In the pagan period, it fuelled wild Bacchanalia, but as Rome moved toward Christianity, it was to form the centre of the Church's principal ceremony in the Communion cup.

Seafood in Leek Sauce

In the original recipe, Apicius calls for liquamen but salt can be used instead

500g / 1lb 2oz oily fish
(e.g. sardines, salmon, mackerel, tuna)
3 tbsp olive oil
250ml / 9fl oz white wine
3 leeks, trimmed and sliced
500ml / 18fl oz fish stock
1 tbsp flour
3 tbsp chopped herbs
(e.g. parsley, coriander, oregano)
Salt and pepper, to taste

Clean the fish and break it into pieces, discarding the bones and the skin. Add the oil, wine, leeks and stock and bring gently to a boil and simmer for around 15 minutes. Stir in the flour then add herbs and seasoning.

Dates stuffed with almonds

Stuffed Dates

This recipe clearly demonstrates how the Romans enjoyed sweet and spicy tastes together

200g / 7oz fresh dates
50g / 1³/4oz chopped nuts (e.g. pine nuts, almonds, walnuts)
Salt and pepper
2 tbsp honey
250ml / 9fl oz red wine

Split open the dates, remove the stones and fill three-quarters of them with the nuts. With the remaining quarter, put in a good pinch of black ground pepper. Place all of the dates on a baking tray and sprinkle with salt. Melt the honey in the wine and pour over. Place in the oven on a medium heat for about 20 minutes.

Roman Boiled Eggs

These eggs are not eaten out of egg cups but served with a spicy sauce as an hors-d'œuvre

8 medium boiled eggs (about 4 minutes, the yolks should still be a bit runny)
50g / 1³/₄oz pine kernels
Honey, salt, vinegar, freshly ground black pepper, to taste

Cut the eggs into halves. Mix together all the other ingredients and pour over the eggs.

Spicy Lamb

This recipe would have used liquamen, which of course, has a very salty but also somewhat fishy taste. Here, salt has been substituted

8 lamb cutlets
2 onions, diced
1 stick of celery, finely sliced
2 tbsp ground coriander
1 tsp ground cumin
1 tsp freshly ground black pepper
3 tbsp olive oil
300ml / ¹/₂ pint white wine mixed with 200ml / 7 fl oz water
Salt, to taste

Put the cutlets in an ovenproof pot with the onion, celery, spices, oil and wine. Cover and cook in a moderate oven for 45 minutes. Take out of the oven, remove the cutlets and boil the sauce to reduce to about a third. If it does not thicken, add a little flour. Add salt, to taste, and pour over the cutlets to serve.

Spices were an important form of flavouring in an otherwise bland diet and their differing prices reflected social status in Roman times and beyond.

First Catch Your Dormouse

The Romans were famous for unusual dishes – ostriches, rats doused in honey, and peacocks, for instance, all featured on a banquet menu. But one of the most popular was baked dormice. These are such tiny creatures they hardly seem worth the effort, but they were considered a great delicacy and would be stuffed with minced pork, herbs and pine nuts, rolled in poppy seeds, sewn up and baked. The image conjured of trying to catch the dormice is amusing, but they were in fact bred and specially fattened for the table, much as guinea pigs are today in some South American countries.

Sweet Roman Toast

While the Romans would have started with flat bread (like pitta bread), this recipe can be adapted to use slices from an ordinary loaf with the crusts removed. It is similar in taste to French toast. With the addition of a few raisins and sultanas, followed by baking in the oven for 15 minutes, it turns into bread and butter pudding

Slices of bread with the crusts removed
Milk, to dip
2 tbsp olive oil
Liquid honey

Remove the crusts from the bread, and slice it. Dip it in the milk and fry in olive oil. Drizzle honey over the top and serve.

DRESSING FOR DINNER

For the Romans, dinner parties were special occasions and guests were greeted with copious hospitality that could take many forms. Petronius wrote in AD 60 of a dinner party – Trimalchio's feast – where the guests were first rubbed down with oil. They were then given their 'dinner clothes', which were the norm in good society. The tunic and shawl, known as a *synthesis* (literally 'combination') could be in warm wool for winter or cooler linen in the summer. Like the ancient Greeks, Romans also liked to wear a wreath on their heads for formal functions (and sometimes informal ones). They could be made of flowers or leaves and were usually scented with oils, and were thought to ward off the effects of too much wine. The Romans even had special shops where craftsmen would produce suitable headgear for party-goers.

The ideal number of guests for a small dinner party was nine, in honour of the nine Muses. They would be arranged around three sides of a square, the fourth open so that the servants could bring the food and clear away. Petronius clearly enjoyed his dinner. After having his hands washed by a slave using icy water, it began with the first course of party food (dormice, olives, sausages) laid out in extravagant bronze dishes. It continued with, in Pertronius' words, 'A hare tricked out with wings to look like Pegasus, a wild sow with a belly full of life thrushes and roast pork carved into models of fish, song birds and a goose. As for the wine, we were fairly swimming in it.'

All meat was expensive in Roman times which meant that every part was used when an animal was slaughtered. Nothing was wasted, even the blood would be turned into black pudding.

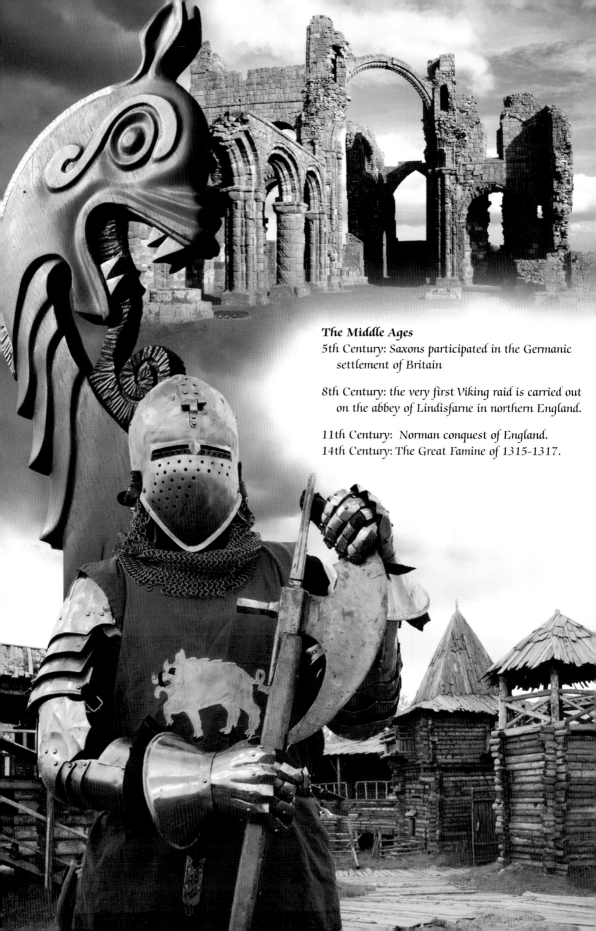

The Middle Ages

5th Century: Saxons participated in the Germanic
    settlement of Britain

8th Century: the very first Viking raid is carried out
    on the abbey of Lindisfarne in northern England.

11th Century: Norman conquest of England.
14th Century: The Great Famine of 1315-1317.

Chapter 3

The Middle Ages

AFTER the fall of the Roman Empire, Europe descended into the Dark Ages, and from this time all the way through to the Renaissance (almost a thousand years) the food people ate and the way that they ate it was governed by three things: the seasons, geography and the Church. Most food was eaten very close to the place it was found, grown or raised. At a time when the horse and cart was the most sophisticated form of transport available and when there were limited means of food preservation, many foodstuffs would have had a very short shelf-life. Fish fresh from the sea would be unknown to those who did not live close to the coast, and milk would travel no further than the next village before it soured.

The Darkest Ages

From the end of Roman influence to the Norman invasion in 1066, England was repeatedly invaded by Angles, Saxons, Jutes and Vikings. This was very much the Dark Ages, a period of wars and raids, isolation and poverty. Other than a few monastic outposts, there were no centres of learning or culture and no great towns. Life was a hand-to-mouth existence, a struggle for survival. Farming continued, albeit primitively, and the diet, especially of the poor, was unsurprisingly extremely limited. Grains were grown – wheat for bread, barley for beer, and oats for porridge and for the animals. Root vegetables such as small red carrots and parsnips were grown, though of course potatoes were still unknown. Onions, leeks and wild garlic were also cultivated and used as flavourings.

Fish from rivers were an important food source as were, but to a lesser degree, fish and shellfish from the sea, being preserved by smoking and salting. Sheep were raised both for their meat and for wool for clothes and blankets, and goats were kept too. Poultry – chickens, geese and ducks – were common, used both for their eggs and their meat. Venison, wild boar, hares and game birds such as grouse and various wild ducks, were all hunted for their meat. When an animal was slaughtered, no part was left unused. The blood from pigs was made into black pudding (with the addition of some herbs and cereal), some of the meat would be preserved by salting for later use and even the animal fat was saved to make tallow for candles.

Most cooking was done over an open fire: either in a cauldron to cook stews and soups (pottage) or, when meat was available, on a spit. Bread was cooked in a clay oven or on a flat dish on the fire. There were also ovens constructed outside the home and made of clay or turf.

Even in these unpredictable times, feasts would continue to take place. As well as quantities of meat and fish, rich pastries and sauces, there was plenty to drink – fruit wines, beer and mead – and there was entertainment in the form of minstrels and story-tellers, jesters and acrobats.

THE SEASONAL AND THE SACRED

Most food would be eaten as it came to fruition, or as it was slaughtered. And many animals would be slaughtered before the winter set in. The main reason for this was the lack of fodder to feed them through to the spring but the practice also chimed in nicely with the Christmas feasts that had taken over from the original pagan winter festivals based on the turning of the year after the shortest day. Any meat remaining after the celebrations would be salted, as other than drying and salting there was no way that it could be preserved or stored. For almost a millennium then, all food was of necessity local and seasonal.

Between the Christmas feasts and the coming of spring, which brought with it the renewal of food sources, came the long fast of Lent. Being the leanest period of the year when food stores were at their lowest, this was fortuitous. It was by no means, though, the only fast imposed by the Church. There were frequent and varying fasts throughout the year: days when no meat could be eaten, other days when both meat and fish were forbidden. The poor, in fact, rarely tasted meat and subsisted mostly on vegetables, soups and grains made into a kind of porridge. Occasionally, game might boost their protein intake but this generally came as a result of poaching – an offence that was usually punished ruthlessly by the local landowner. The lower classes did keep pigs as they could forage in the forests and did not depend on fodder being provided. And if you were a comparatively wealthy peasant, you might even have a cow, in which case dairy products would form a good part of your diet. Ultimately, however it was the thick soup known as pottage that was the daily fare – and the rich ate it regularly too. Its ingredients could include meat, vegetables and cereals. The cereal version was known as 'frumenty', while the meatier version was called 'mortrew'.

For the wealthy, however, feasts were not just for Christmas. They had to observe the periods of fasting (though there were some clever ways of boosting your diet even then), but when it came to feasting they certainly knew how to throw a party, and at banquets no expense was spared. They were firm believers in the 'nothing succeeds like excess' school of cuisine. At King Richard's feast

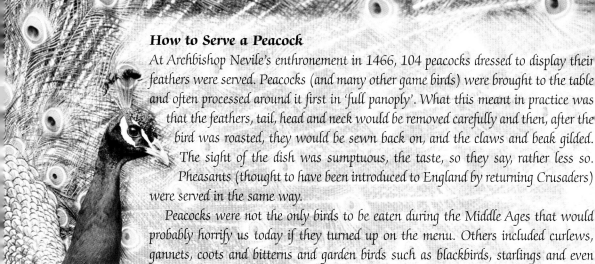

How to Serve a Peacock

At Archbishop Nevile's enthronement in 1466, 104 peacocks dressed to display their feathers were served. Peacocks (and many other game birds) were brought to the table and often processed around it first in 'full panoply'. What this meant in practice was that the feathers, tail, head and neck would be removed carefully and then, after the bird was roasted, they would be sewn back on, and the claws and beak gilded. The sight of the dish was sumptuous, the taste, so they say, rather less so.

Pheasants (thought to have been introduced to England by returning Crusaders) were served in the same way.

Peacocks were not the only birds to be eaten during the Middle Ages that would probably horrify us today if they turned up on the menu. Others included curlews, gannets, coots and bitterns and garden birds such as blackbirds, starlings and even little sparrows. Larks were mostly eaten by the poor, served up like toad-in-the-hole but with birds in the batter instead of sausages.

The Archbishop's banquet also featured 300 tuns of ale, 100 tuns of wine (a tun was equivalent to 2 butts = 4 hogsheads = 252 gallons), 1 pipe of hippocras, 104 oxen, 6 wild bulls, 1,000 sheep, 304 calves, 2,000 pigs, 400 swans, 2,000 geese, 1,000 capons, 13,500 other birds, 500 stags, 1,500 venison pies, 600 pike and bream, 12 porpoises and seals, and 13,000 dishes of sweetmeats, including custards, jellies and tarts. There were, though, around 6,000 guests!

on 23 September 1387 there were boars' heads, roasted swans and pigs, venison and 'custarde lumbarde' (see MEDIEVAL COOKBOOKS P43), and that was just the first of three courses. Unlike our modern tradition of courses, in which savoury is followed by sweet, in the Middle Ages, all the tastes were mixed up together. The second course, therefore, was not dissimilar to the first, featuring soups, roasted pigs, cranes, pheasants, herons, rabbits, chickens and some fish (bream). The final course had yet more roasted venison, chickens and rabbits, quails and larks, with a few sweeter dishes too, such as 'Payne Puff', a pie containing egg yolks, bone marrow, dates, raisins and ginger.

All this game was acquired as a result of the chase, hunting being the favourite pastime of the wealthy. Between 24 June and 14 September they hunted deer. The rest of the time they hunted wild boar with dogs, swords, spears, and bows and arrows. They used hawks to hunt for bigger game birds. It was not just gentlemen who enjoyed hunting and hawking, ladies did too, in spite of the Church frequently condemning it as a brutal activity. On the other hand, the case for hunting was made by Edward, Duke of York, in the early Fifteenth Century in *The Master of the Game*:

> For when the hunter riseth in the morning, and he sees a sweet and fair morn and clear weather and bright, and he heareth the song of the small birds, the which sing so sweetly with great melody and full of love, each in its own language in the best wise … and that is great joy and liking to the hunter's heart. After when he shall go to his quest or searching, he shall see or meet anon with the hart without great seeking, and shall harbour him well and readily within a little compass. And when he has come home he shall doff his clothes and his shoes and his hose, and he shall wash his thighs and his legs, and peradventure all his body. And in the meanwhile he shall order well his supper, with the neck of the hart and of other good meats and good wine or ale. And then he shall go and drink and lie in his bed in fair fresh clothes, and shall sleep well and

Realistic delicacies

It wasn't just what people ate in the Middle Ages, it was how they served it that we would find deeply unappealing today. Many children now assume that meat is something that just appears in the supermarket refrigerator as a portion wrapped in cellophane on a plastic tray – they have never seen it any other way. But our ancestors were fully aware of the origins of their food, how it was killed and exactly what it was they were eating. It was, therefore, not only the peacocks that would be presented as closely as possible to the way they had looked when alive, hares would be sat on their haunches and the feet of tiny birds would appear through pie crust. The hog's head – a real delicacy – would be paraded on its platter, grinning horribly at the company.

Sweet Tastes

Until Tudor times, honey was the main sweetener that was generally available. Besides sweetening food, it was also used for the alcoholic drink of mead. The people in Medieval times had a sweet tooth and sweet dishes were popular. Chaucer mentions trifle, a rich pudding made with lashings of cream and ground almonds. But some dishes that sound like puddings actually contained meat too. Blancmange was a popular sweet dish of the Middle Ages, though it was unexpectedly made with ground almonds and minced capons.

Our Daily Bread

The daily bread of the Lord's Prayer actually means daily food, but it demonstrates how bread was recognised as such a fundamental part of the diet. A large slab of it was used instead of a plate. This was known as the trencher and could have a slightly hollowed out surface to avoid spillages. The bread was actually around four days old and stale, but it made a good cutting surface and, when you finished eating, you threw the remaining sauce-sodden crusts to the dogs – or kept it for the next day's plate.

How to Cook Your Ox

By far the most popular cooking method of the period was roasting on a spit over an open fire. This was uncomplicated, if exhausting for the turner, and the method could be used for everything from oxen to pheasants. Care had to be taken to ensure that the meat did not dry out. The juices that dripped from the meat were constantly poured back over it as a baste. And sometimes, if a gilded effect was desired, a special baste that included egg yolks, flour and the golden spice of saffron could be used instead.

steadfastly all the night without any evil thoughts of any sins, wherefore I say that hunters go into Paradise when they die, and live in this world more joyfully than any other man.

Most large meat and game would be cooked on a spit over a fire. But other forms of cooking included jugging, particularly for hare and pheasant. This entailed jointing the meat and placing the joints in a pot with flavourings such as spices, onions and stock. This would then be tightly covered and placed in a deeper pan of boiling water and cooked slowly. The joints would then be removed and a rich sauce made from the remaining ingredients.

Venison was the meat of choice in the Medieval period. The rich hunted it and the poor poached it — often with fatal consequences if caught. It must, though, have been all too tempting for them as great herds of deer roamed the forests at that time.

Drying fish was a popular method of preservation and ensured that fish could be eaten more than a couple of days after it had been caught.

Cod Wars

At the end of the Fifteenth Century, the first international cod war broke out. Cod fishing began on a large scale around Newfoundland, and the English, French, Dutch and Basque fishing fleets were all were protected by their national navies. The Basques were driven out first as they had the least powerful navy. The three remaining powers shared out the cod between them, but they all had the problem of how to preserve the fish before it reached its consumers. Salting took place on board the fishing craft or back on the nearest land, and sometimes fast sailing ships were on hand to get the fish back quickly. The ships set out equipped with salt and they had large holds – cod is bulky rather than heavy. In northern France, the little port of Olonne near La Rochelle sent out up to a hundred sailing ships and several thousand men to the other side of the Atlantic every year. There was a race to be the first ship back as the winner could expect to earn twice as much as the later vessels, weight for weight of fish, such was the clamour for the new catch.

Soteletees

Each of the three courses served at King Richard's magnificent feast in September 1387 was accompanied by a 'soteltee' or 'subtlety'. There was nothing subtle about them, however, as they were huge food sculptures and they were served as a centrepiece – no great banquet would be complete without them. They could take many forms such as castles or ships, but would also, rather like the masques that formed part of the entertainment, have a symbolic or mythological character.

MEDIEVAL COOKBOOKS

Surprisingly, there are a few hand written medieval cookbooks that have survived to the present today, however, their instructions bear little resemblance to contemporary cookery books, giving no measurements or quantities or cooking times. They do, though, give detailed information about preparation (grinding, chopping, straining, scalding), flavourings and how to alter recipes to take into account the age of the meat, or how to make a dish acceptable during Lent. Some of the manuscripts that can be found in the British Library include:

- A Boke of Kokery, which was written around 1440 and includes a recipe for 'custarde lumbarde' (which put in an appearance at King Richard's famous 1387 feast). The custarde (also known as crustade) was an open pie containing cream, eggs and dates

- The Forme of Cury is thought to have been written by King Richard's master cook at the end of the Fourteenth Century. The manuscript emphasises the link between food and medicine and has recipes for 'common potages' (soups) and elaborate dishes for banquets. 'Cury' is the Middle English word for 'cookery'

- Potage Dyvers was written between 1430 and 1440 and features recipes for 'capoun in Salome' (spiced capon) and 'pompys' (meatballs)

A TASTE FOR SPICE

All over the continent of Europe as well as in Britain, much of the food in the Middle Ages was seasoned with spices and contained imported fruits. This was partly a continuation of the Roman tradition and, given the age of some of the meat and fish that was consumed, they no doubt did much to improve the flavour. There was an added interest in these exotic foods too, as the Crusades had opened up once more the riches of the Levant and the Mediterranean, which had been all but cut off during the Dark Ages. Returning knights brought back entirely new foods – pheasants are believed to have arrived in Britain with homecoming Crusaders – and also spices from the Orient.

The more of these treasures you could display on your table, the greater was your prestige. And treasures were the only way to describe them. Such exotic commodities as pepper, saffron, caraway, nutmeg, ginger, raisins, dates, figs and almonds were alarmingly expensive, and their price reflected not only their rarity but also the long and dangerous overland journey from their countries of origin. The demand for them a few centuries later would trigger the voyages of discovery, looking for a sea route to the luxuries of the East.

Nevertheless, recipes of the time demanded spices. *Le Menagier de Paris* (1393) had a recipe for black pudding that required 'ginger, clove and a little pepper'. Spices were also taken in the form of preserved fruits and medicinal powders against a whole array of diseases.

Spices were an important form of flavouring in an otherwise bland diet and their differing prices reflected social status in Roman times and beyond.

The Cup That Cheers

Eleanor of Aquitaine was not only a great supporter of the Crusades, she went on one herself, accompanying her husband Louis VII of France and taking with her the knights of Aquitaine and many of her ladies in waiting. After the French king's death she swiftly married Henry II of England and, as the richest heiress of her day, brought many lands with her. The marriage was not a happy one – Henry had his queen imprisoned for 15 years – but Aquitaine itself was to provide England with good French wine, not only during Eleanor's time, but into the reigns of her sons and theirs for many years to come.

Brandy was also available, made by distilling wine, but used generally as a medicine. The first such distillation was thought to have taken place in the Twelfth Century. One doctor who recommended brandy for its medicinal properties was Arnaud de Villeneuve who taught in Montpellier and Paris. He wrote a work called *La conservation de la jeunesse*, because among its virtues was supposedly the preservation of youth, along with benefits for the heart, ague and toothache. His miracle cure brought Charles the Bad to a bad end indeed in 1387. He was sewn into a brandy soaked sheet, but a servant holding a candle to check his sewing sent his master up in flames.

More humble and less exciting drinking took place in the alehouse, not to be confused with the more salubrious tavern or inn where wine might be served. Wine soared in price during the Middle Ages. At the beginning of the Fourteenth Century it cost 3d a gallon, but by the Fifteenth it was 8d and a hundred years later around 2s 8d. Even ale was not cheap. In 1266 the Assize of Ale fixed the price at $1/2$d a gallon but this rose to $1^{1}/2$d in 1283 and it was still not of particularly good quality, described by one drinker of the time as 'muddy, foggy, fulsome, puddle, stinking'.

SALT AND SEATING PLANS

Salt was a highly prized commodity even in ancient times. In the Middle Ages, it defined your place in the world – whether you sat above or below the salt at the table. It was treated with the greatest respect and had its own special container, the salt cellar, which became increasingly elaborate over the centuries, sometimes given the shape of a ship with wheels that could glide it along to the diners. In the Medieval period, the salt would be placed on the high table, in the centre and opposite the host. This in itself was a measure of his prestige.

Precedence was everything at Medieval dinners. Everyone was seated in accordance with rank and the high table – reserved for the host and favoured guests – had the all important salt cellar. Everyone else sat 'below the salt' and the further you were from it, the lowlier your station and the less generous your dinner. Royals took pride of place, followed by the princes of the Church and the aristocracy, and the marshal or usher would be there to oversee that everyone was in the right place.

Even when finally seated, diners at a Medieval banquet did not immediately begin to eat. In many European countries, food would be tasted first by servants to check that it was not poisoned. This could take some time (poison may not have an immediate effect) and the unfortunate tasters were supposed to do their possibly fatal job with grace and an apparent lack of concern. They also had various tools, substances that would indicate the presence of poison, and these took such diverse shapes as crystals and parts of rare animals such as rhinoceros or perhaps unicorn horns. There would then often be a speech before the hungry guests could fall to. Although there were huge quantities of food at banquets, it was arranged along the tables and you were expected to eat only what was closest to you. Generally speaking, you would not get the chance to even try all of the dishes. You were expected to help serve your neighbours and as a particular sign of favour, you could send little tasters of a dish down to a friend.

The tables – even the high table, or high borde – were narrow, being

Worth its Salt

The phrase 'worth its salt' is derived from meat curing – only the best would be considered worth the expense of salting. Meat could be simply covered in salt or immersed in a salty solution of water for preservation.

designed for diners to sit just on one side. This was to enable everyone to see the king or the lord at his dinner. In later centuries, the great man (or woman) eating became a spectacle that drew crowds. Understandably, some lords preferred a little more solitude. Perhaps it was all the waiting around that prompted some of the nobility to opt for eating alone or with a handful of others in a private room, instead of being on display. This eventually became known as the withdrawing room and, many years later, it evolved into the drawing room.

The tablecloth also became important during the Middle Ages. It had been around since Roman times, but in the Medieval period it gained a new significance. Only the most important people at the table received a tablecloth or a part of it. The cloths were already generally white – no doubt as a proof of their cleanliness – and so they have remained to this day, especially for formal occasions. Only the wealthy could afford them and several cloths would be laid one on top of the other on a well-dressed table. They could be removed one at a time to coincide with new courses. Napkins appeared too, though they bore little resemblance to the napkins we use today. Generally they were much larger and were worn over the shoulder, and while they could be used for wiping greasy hands, equally so could the tablecloth – though it was considered bad manners to wipe your hands on your clothes.

Knives and spoons were the only implements used at the table and usually the knives were not specifically designed for eating. Any knife would do and you were expected to bring your own rather than expect your host to supply it. Men would use it to cut the meat on the platter, or charger, for themselves and their ladies. Soups and stews in bowls would be shared, along with the spoon, between two or more diners. Your plate was a slice of stale bread – this would afterwards be thrown to the dogs – and fresh bread was provided for the diners to actually eat. From the Fourteenth Century, a wooden or even a pewter trencher began to be used, first to support the bread and eventually to replace it.

When banquets took place in the great hall, there wasn't just food to enjoy, there was entertainment too. There were singing troubadours, jugglers, dancers, and the theatrical and symbolic masques that were to become such a feature of Tudor life. Masques could be based on mythological themes, political alliances (for instance, during a wedding that joined two noble families) or simply feature the exotic – wild animals or tales from the Crusades. In France, there were reports of fountains of wine and children dressed as angels descending from above on cables.

With all this increasing sophistication, it should come as no surprise that some thought was given to table manners. Accordingly, special courtesy books began to appear, advising diners who wanted to be invited again to avoid farting, scratching their flea bites and picking their noses.

Fruit and Flowers

Many of the fruits or varieties of fruits that people enjoyed in the Middle Ages have become extinct. The Medieval Englishman might enjoy apples such as costard or pomewater, pearmain, russetting and Apple-John. Codlin, meaning small unripe apples, was taken by Dickens as the name for his character in *The Old Curiosity Shop*, who did love his food (see page 129-130). And the apples would be used not just in pies and sauces but for cider, one of the most popular varieties for this being the pippin – one apple (usually Cox's Orange Pippin) that we still have today. However, all fruit and vegetables were cooked as it was believed that eaten raw, they caused disease. *The Boke of Kervynge* (Book of Carving) written in 1500 warns: 'Beware of green sallettes and rawe fruytes for they wyll make your soverayne seke.' (Beware of green salads and raw fruits for they will make your lord sick.)

Herb gardens were an important feature in the Medieval manor house, and flowers were regarded as equally important both for culinary and medicinal purposes. According to Alexander Neckham in his *De Naturis Rerum* in the early Thirteenth Century:

> The garden should be adorned with roses and lilies, the turnsole or heliotrope, violets and mandrake, there you should have parsley, cost, fennel, southernwood, coriander, sage, savory, hyssop, mint, rue, ditanny, smallage, pellitory, lettuce, garden cress and peonies. There should also be beds planted with onions, leeks, garlic, pumpkins and shallots. The cucumber, the poppy, the daffodil, and brank-ursine ought to be in a good garden. There should also be pottage herbs, such as beets, herb mercury, orach, sorrel and mallows.

Roses were used for their colour, flavour and scent in dishes in the Middle Ages.

Brie, a Cheese Fit For a King

In France, cheese dates back to the earliest monastic farms. One particularly famous French cheese was brie. The curd would be renneted and aired, shovelled into a flat mould with straw on its base, drained, decanted, salted, turned and matured. Charlemagne sampled it in 774, being instructed by the monks to eat it whole, including the crust. It was an immediate hit and he ordered two batches to be sent to Aachen every year.

Later, it was shipped to Paris by the River Marne and was a royal favourite enjoyed by, amongst others, Charles VIII, Henri IV and, to his misfortune, Louis XVI – who was finally executed after being caught in Varennes, having fled from Paris, because he dallied over his brie in a tavern and was recognised by the village postmaster Drouet.

MEDIEVAL COOKBOOK

Baked Mallard

Ducks of all kinds were a popular dish in the Middle Ages. This is a modernised version of a typically spicy Medieval dish (with thanks to Daniel Myers for the recipes in this section)

3–4 medium onions
1/4 cup verjuice (grape juice with a sour taste)
1 duck (900g–1.3kg / 2–3lb), de-boned and cut into pieces
1/4 tsp salt
1/4 tsp pepper
1/8 tsp cloves
1/8 tsp mace
2 tbsp butter
450g / 1lb shortcrust pastry
1 tsp chopped parsley
1/4 tsp thyme

Grind the onions with a mortar and pestle (or in a food processor), add the verjuice, and strain out the solids, reserving the liquid. In a large bowl, mix the duck, salt, pepper, cloves, mace, butter, and the onion/verjuice liquid. Place the mixture into pie crusts and sprinkle with parsley and thyme. Cover with the top crust and bake at 180°C / 350°F / gas mark 4 until done (about an hour).

Source: *The Good Housewife's Jewell*, T. Dawson: To bake a Mallard. Take three or foure Onyons, and stampe them in a morter, then straine them with a saucer full of vergice, then take your mallard and put him into the iuyce of the sayde onyons, and season him with pepper, and salte, cloves and mace, then put your Mallard into the coffin with the saide juyce of the onyons, and a good quantity of Winter-savorye, a little tyme, and perselye chopped small, and sweete Butter, so close it up and bake it.

Stewed Venison

A middle-Dutch recipe for stewed venison. This is an easy and reasonably quick dish to make. The cooking broth makes a perfect sauce when strained and thickened with bread crumbs

    900g / 2lb venison steaks
    4 strips bacon
    2 cups red wine
    1 cup water
    1 tsp cinnamon
    1 tsp ginger
    Pinch of saffron, ground

Cut the venison and bacon into small pieces. Place into a large pot with the remaining ingredients. Bring to the boil and simmer for about 20 minutes.

Source: *Wel ende edelike spijse* (Good and noble food), Christianne Muusers (trans.): *.viij. Venysoen herten ende hynden ghesneden by sneden wel ghelaerdeert al rau siedet in vele wijns ende lettel waters laert daerin ghesneden soffraen ginge bare Caneele daer in ghenouch*

Roast game. Deer and hind, cut in pieces (?), well larded while still raw. Cook it in a lot of wine and a little water, [with] chopped bacon [and] sufficient saffron, ginger and cinnamon.

Baked Fish

The following recipe makes a wonderfully light dish that is excellent served over rice (though, of course, it would not have been originally)

  4 perch fillets
  $^1/_2$ cup red wine
  $^1/_2$ cup water
  $^1/_2$ slice bread, ground
  $^1/_8$ cup sugar
  Olive oil
  Salt
  Pepper
  Cloves
  Mace

Rinse the perch fillets, place in a baking dish and bake at 180°C / 350°F / gas mark 4 for 15–20 minutes. Put the wine, water, bread crumbs, and sugar into a saucepan and bring to a boil. Reduce to a medium heat and simmer for about 20 minutes.

Remove the fish from the baking dish and pan-fry it in olive oil for about 10 minutes. Sprinkle with salt, pepper, cloves and mace to taste. Serve hot, topped with the wine sauce.

Source: *Two Fifteenth-Century Cookery-Books*, Thomas Gloning (ed.): Salomene. Take gode Wyne, an gode pouder, & Brede y-ground, an sugre, an boyle it y-fere; than take Trowtys, Rochys, Perchys, other Carpys, other alle these y-fere, an make hem clene, & aftere roste hem on a Grydelle; than hewe hem in gobettys: whan they ben y-sothe, fry hem in oyle a lytil, then caste in the brwet; and whan thou dressist it, take Maces, Clowes, Quybibes, Gelofrys; an cast a-boue, & serue forth.

Veal Pie

This recipe is a bit unusual for the modern palate, again combining meat with sweet, spicy flavours. The original source called for an extra pound of beef fat, which has been left out to make it a bit more healthy

350g / 12oz veal
3 eggs
1 cup cream
1 tsp cinnamon
1 tsp nutmeg
2 tbsp sugar
1/4 tsp salt
450g / 1lb shortcrust pastry

Bake the veal in a covered dish for about 45 minutes at 180°C / 350°F / gas mark 4. Let it cool and then chop it into fine pieces. Set aside.

Beat the eggs in a large bowl. Add the cream and spices and mix well. Add the chopped veal to the mixture and pour into the pie shell. Cover with the top crust and bake at 180°C / 350°F / gas mark 4 until done – about an hour. Serve warm or at room temperature.

Source: *Ouverture de Cuisine*, Thomas Gloning (ed.): Pour faire tourtes de veau à la creme. Prennez douze onces de chair de veau, & la faites cuire, puis prennez demye liure de graisse de boeuf, & hachez tout ensemble, battez trois oeufs cruds, quatre onces de succre, demye once de canelle, vne noix muscade, vn peu de sel, demye sopine de creme, bien meslé tout ensemble, & faites vostre tourte selon vostre fantasie.

Source: Ouverture de Cuisine, Daniel Myers (trans.)]: To make veal tarts with cream. Take twelve ounces of veal, & do it to cook, then take a half pound of beef fat, & chop all together, beat three raw eggs, four ounces sugar, half an ounce of cinnamon, a nutmeg, a little salt, half a sopine of cream, mix well all together, & make your tart as you please.

Nutmeg was a desirable but costly spice in the Middle Ages and would denote the status of its user.

Both the nutmeg and its outer skin mace were valued commodities for the Middle Ages' kitchen and boudoir as mace was also used as a perfume, not just a flavoursome spice.

Coney in Civey

The original animal fat 'freysshe grece' has been replaced, for modern palates, with olive oil

> 1.8kg / 4lb chicken, rabbit, or duck, cut into $2^1/_2$ cm / 1in squares
> 2 tbsp olive oil
> 1 medium onion, chopped
> 1 cup red wine
> 2 cups chicken broth
> $^1/_2$ tsp mace
> $^1/_4$ tsp cloves
> $^1/_2$ tsp black pepper
> $^1/_4$ tsp cinnamon (canelle)
> 1 cup bread crumbs (2 slices)
> $^1/_4$ tsp ginger
> $^1/_4$ cup red wine vinegar
> $^1/_4$ tsp salt

Sear pieces of meat briefly in a large pot and set aside, using olive oil as necessary. Sauté the onions in the remaining oil until tender. Return the meat to the pot and add wine, broth, mace, cloves, pepper and cinnamon. Bring to the boil and simmer for one hour. Add bread crumbs, ginger, vinegar and salt just before serving.

Source: Two Fifteenth-Century Cookery-Books, T. Austin (ed.): .xlij. Conyng, Mawlard, in gely or in cyuey. Take Conynge, Hen, or Mawlard, and roste hem alle-most y-now, or ellys choppe hem, an frye hem in fayre Freysshe grece; an frye myncyd Oynenons, and caste alle in-to the potte, & caste ther-to fayre Freysshe brothe, an half Wyne, Maces, Clowes, Powder pepir, Canelle; than take fayre Brede, an wyth the same brothe stepe, an draw it thorw a straynoure wyth vynegre; an whan it is wyl y-boylid, caste the lycoure ther to, & powder Gyngere, & Salt, & sesyn it vp an serue forth.

Quince Jelly

This recipe is very easy, but it is also very time consuming. You can spread the work out over a couple of days by baking the quince and refrigerating it, leaving the simmering for the next day

   1.13kg / 2 ½lb quince (about 6 cups)
   2 cups water
   1.13kg / 2 ½lb sugar (5 cups)

Peel and core the quince. Cut them into small (less than 1cm / ½in) pieces and put them in an oven-safe baking dish along with the water and half the sugar. Cover and bake at 180°C / 350°F / gas mark 4 until soft – about an hour and a half. Drain, keeping the liquid, and mash the quince. Then put the liquid, quince pulp, and remaining sugar into a large pan and bring to a low boil. Simmer, stirring constantly, until mixture becomes very thick. You should be able to scrape the spoon across the pan and see the bottom. Ladle into wide-mouth jars, cool and set.

Source: Catherine Tolmach's *Receipts of Pastery, Confectionary, & cetera*. To make rough red marmelade of Quinces. Take Quinces and pare them, cut them in small peces from the coare, then take as much sugar as the peces doe waye, and put the Quinces beinge cutt into an erthen pott and put halfe the sugar that you waied into the pott and as much water as will couer them, then sett them into an ouen with howsholde breade. then when they are paked poore them into a postnett or preseruinge pan and put the rest of the sugar to it, then bruse them with the back of a spoone, then boyle them with sturringe till it will come cleane from the bottome of the pan then boxe it.

Turnip (Rapes) Pottage

Pre-cooking the turnips for this simple vegetable soup reduces the natural bite of the turnips and keeps them from being too strong, leaving a pleasant, warming flavour

4–5 turnips, peeled and cut into 1cm / $^1/_2$ in cubes
$^1/_2$ medium onion, chopped
2 cups chicken broth
$^1/_4$ tsp salt
$^1/_2$ tsp powder douce (see opposite)
Pinch of saffron

Put the turnips into a pot with enough water to cover them. Bring to a boil and allow to simmer until they start to soften – about 10 minutes. Drain and add the remaining ingredients. Return to the boil, reduce the heat, and continue to cook until done. Serve hot.

Source: *The Forme of Cury*. Take rapus and make hem clene and waissh hem clene. quare hem. Parboile hem. Take hem up. Cast hem in a gode broth and see? hem. Mynce Oynouns and cast ?erto Safroun and salt and messe it forth with powdour douce. the wise make of Pasturnakes and skyrwates.

Powder Douce (Sweet)

Many Medieval recipes call for spice mixtures without detailing the exact spices. While it is tempting to assume that each particular spice mixture had a consistent recipe, there is evidence of substantial variation for different times, regions, budgets and cooks

 1½ tbsp cinnamon
 1 tsp cloves
 3 tbsp ginger
 1 tsp nutmeg
 2 tbsp sugar

Mix the ingredients.

Source: *Le Menagier de Paris*, Janet Hinson (trans.): HIPPOCRAS. To make powdered hippocras, take a quarter-ounce of very fine cinnamon, hand-picked by tasting it, an ounce of very fine meche ginger and an ounce of grains of paradise, a sixth of an ounce of nutmeg and galingale together, and pound it all together. And when you want to make hippocras, take a good half-ounce or more of this powder and two quarter-ounces of sugar, and mix them together, and a quart of wine as measured in Paris. And note that the powder and the sugar mixed together make 'duke's powder'.

Note: Grains of paradise are the seeds from Aframomum melegueta, sometimes known as melegueta pepper or guinea pepper. They are smaller and harder than black peppercorns, and have a flavour somewhere between pepper and cardamom.

Medieval Foodie-isms

High borde – High table

Ewerer – Servant who carries the water bowl to the table for hand
          washing between courses

Pantner – Servant who serves bread (from the French, *pain*)

Trencher – Stale bread used as a plate and cutting surface by diners

Cury – Cookery

Frumenty – Cereal based pottage (soup)

Mortrew – Meat-based pottage

Custarde or crustade – An open pie

Hippocras – A sweet liqueur from the eastern Mediterranean

The Sixteenth Century:

1501: Michelangelo returns to his native
Florence to begin work on the statue David.

1577-80: Francis Drake circles the World.

1589 - Sir Walter Raleigh first brought the
potato to Ireland and England

Chapter 4

The
Sixteenth Century

A FTER a millennium when food and cooking remained essentially the same, during the reigns of the Tudors the English saw great changes at their tables. New foods were imported from the Continent and by Elizabeth I's reign they came from the New World too. Potatoes, chocolate, coffee and tea were highly prized novelties, but it wasn't all good news. Tobacco made its first appearance, while sugar replaced honey for the rich – resulting in horribly rotten teeth at court. By the end of her reign, Elizabeth's teeth were black. Many members of the court also suffered from scurvy as the rich disdained vegetables – they were only fit for the poor – and for the same reason they were prone to hideous skin eruptions. The lack of vitamin A in the courtiers' diet often led to painful kidney and bladder conditions. And, of course, while obesity was a condition that would never afflict the vast poor majority, the Tudors provided us with one of the most famous fat men in history. Henry VIII changed from the athletic figure of his youth, when he was rated the most handsome monarch in Europe, to the elephantine king portrayed by Holbein and his imitators.

GOOD KING HENRY'S KITCHEN

While some of the screen portrayals of Henry VIII have perhaps somewhat exaggerated his gluttony and appalling manners, the image of him gnawing on great shanks of meat is not such an unlikely one. The Tudors had an extremely high protein diet with lots of meat and game. Deer, boar, rabbit, quail, beef, mutton, veal, lamb, kid, pork, rabbit, pheasant, partridge, chicken, duck, swan, peacock, goose and pigeon would all appear regularly on the table. Henry's kitchen at Hampton Court Palace produced food on a colossal scale, feeding as it needed to, around 600 people twice a day. Much of this original kitchen has been restored so that visitors today can see how it was done, though in fact, this kitchen did not provide Henry's own dinners, as he had a private kitchen for himself and his inner circle.

The kitchens were overpoweringly hot and manning them was hard work. The spits on which oxen, deer and virtually all other meats were roasted were very heavy, and it is now believed that they were not turned by children, as was once thought, but by adult men. The original kitchens and stores covered a colossal area – 36,000 square feet or 3,350 square metres – and comprised not just the kitchens themselves but stores, quality control centres and an accounts department. The Board of the Green Cloth was in overall charge and also kept an eagle eye on pilfering.

There were blocks that contained live animals. Most would be delivered while they were still alive and then butchered in the palace butchery, which was one way of keeping food fresher for longer! There was also a palace bakery, and the wine cellar had ale as well as wine.

THE LISLE LETTERS

One of the most remarkable insights into life in the reign of Henry VIII exists in the form of the letters of the Lisle family. They are still extant for two reasons. First, they were written as a result of Lord Lisle's appointment as Deputy of Calais in 1533 when much of his family and all of his business affairs and estates were in England, and he had to run them from what was then long distance. And second, they were kept because they were used as documentary evidence in Lord Lisle's trial for treason that culminated in his being sent to the Tower of London. For the most part, however, the letters tell the story of everyday Tudor life among the aristocracy, including not only what people ate but also the importance of food as a commodity, a gift and even a way of sealing alliances.

While Lady Lisle travelled to France with her husband, their children were left behind. Their 15-year-old eldest son, John Basset, was left in the care of Richard Norton, a prosperous neighbour to their home in Hampshire and a Justice of the Peace. To him Lady Lisle would send gifts of expensive – and unusual – food. In a letter dated 6 July 1534, Norton wrote to reassure her on her son's account and to thank her for one such gift:

> Madam, ye have cause to yield thanks to God greatly that ye have so towardly a son, for assuredly there is in him many good qualities, like a gentleman concerned to wisdom and learning, and is fully replenished with courtesy, gentleness and kindness. And he shall lack nothing to his comfort and pleasure at all times that may lie in me. I thank your ladyship for your kind remembrance and provision for venison, mews and wine, which mews I have received from James your servant.

A mews, or sea-mews, was a common seagull.

In Calais, soon after his arrival, Lord Lisle strove for good relations with his neighbours – as did they with him. The most important of them was Oudart du Bies, the seneschal of Boulogne. He wrote to Lord Lisle on 2 September 1533:

> I was informed yesterday of a wild boar the which was sighted a league hence; and took thither my greyhounds which did take the same, and it killed me two of the best of them. I send you the head thereof, praying to take this my poor gift in good part. I shall take pains to procure other

greyhounds; and if you find the said boar's head to your taste I pray you inform me, and if I take more you shall have your part therein.

John Husee, familiarly described as 'My Lord Lisle's man', emerges from the letters as the perfect family retainer, handling their affairs in England at every level. He wrote to Lord Lisle on 23 May 1537 on the matter of quails, or so it would seem. In fact, the procurement of the quails (which were nowhere to be found in England) for the Queen (Henry's third wife, Jane Seymour) was also connected with the procurement of a place at court for Lord Lisle's daughter, Anne:

> Sir John Russell [has] wrote to your lordship sundry letters by the King's commandment expressly, and how the very effect of those letters was for fat quails for the Queen's Highness, which her Grace loveth very well and longeth not a little for them … with most speed your lordship send ij or iij dozen and cause them to be killed at Dover; and that in anywise that those same be very fat; and afterwards, as shortly as your lordship may, to send xx or xxx dozen.

A few months later, Anne had her place at court.

Lady Lisle was clearly something of a cook herself. After a visit from Archdeacon Thomas Thirlby in 1538 (on an unsuccessful mission to find a French bride for the King after Jane Seymour's death), she wrote to him with a recipe request:

> Be so good unto your servant and worst scholar as to write unto me of the thing you taught me, how many pound of sugar must go to how many pounds of quinces, barberries, and damsons or plums. I have clean forgotten how many pounds of the one and of the other. Now the time of quinces is come, I would fain be doing.

And she clearly was not such a bad scholar in the kitchen. In 1539 her daughter Anne, now ensconced at court wrote:

> The king doth so well like the conserves you sent him last, that his Grace commanded me to write unto you for more of the codiniac [quince marmalade] of the clearest making, and of the conserve of damsons; and this as soon as may be.

DAILY BREAD AND POTTAGE

In spite of all the novelties that were to arrive during the century, pottage and bread still underpinned the nation's diet. The bread could be made from wheat, rye or barley, and different qualities of bread were consumed at various levels of society. Spiced breads could only be made on Good Friday (like today's Hot Cross Buns) and at Christmas or funerals.

- Manchet was a very fine white bread made from wheat flour, creamy yellow in colour and eaten by the nobility

- Raveled bread was also called Yeoman's bread and was made from coarser wholewheat flour with the bran left in. It was darker in colour and cheaper than manchet

- Carter's bread was dark brown or black and made from a mixture of rye and wheat, or barley and wheat, or just from rye. In the north it could also be made from oats

- Horse corn was a bread that could be made from almost anything – peas, beans, lentils, oats or even acorns – and it was eaten by the poorest people when the harvest failed

Pottage still featured large in the everyday diet. This was probably just as well for reasons of health as it was one of the few times that the wealthy ever came face to face with a vegetable. Vegetables were never served as an accompaniment to meat as they are today and the court generally disdained them as being fit only for the poor. However, those of lesser rank

who lived in the country grew a wide variety of vegetables that would go into the pottage (along with egg yolks, milk, bread crumbs and herbs) or be served as 'sallets', which included not just salads but any dish made from vegetables. Favourites included turnips, broad beans, onions, leeks, garlic, peas, parsnips, carrots, beetroot, artichokes, asparagus, lentils, radishes, Good King Henry (a green vegetable that tasted like spinach) and various types of cabbage.

Herbs were also grown for flavouring pottage and meat dishes, particularly parsley, chives, rosemary, thyme, sage and borage. They could also be used with the 'thresh' – the straw that would be strewn on the floor – to freshen the house. The thresh gave its name to the threshold, with its purpose of holding the thresh within the house. Herbs and vegetables were not the only ingredients found in the garden. Flowers would also be used in 'sallets' – daisies, dandelions, primroses, violets and marigolds were all popular.

Pottage could also contain meat and, for the poor, this was the best way to eke it out. This mainly consisted of chicken and rabbit. Wealthier peasants would also keep a pig – particularly serviceable as it could be left to forage in the forest.

Poaching still carried heavy punishments. If you were caught during the day you might be fined or imprisoned, however, poachers discovered at night would be put to death.

Let Them Eat Salt

At the other end of the social scale, the royal household not only ate large quantities of flesh, but large quantities of salt too. Over three quarters of the diet consisted of meat, from oxen to tiny larks. All preserved food – fish and meat – was stored using salt and it was around the time of the Tudors that this became the favourite taste. Up until this time, food had mostly been highly spiced and sweet and, while both were still popular, by the end of the period, salty foods were beginning to take over.

Shakespeare's Dinners

Shakespeare's plays contain countless references to food and drink. They are not always used in the context of meals, however. Hotspur in *Henry IV Part One* dismisses Glendower thus:

> I cannot choose: sometime he angers me
> With telling me of the moldwarp and the ant,
> Of the dreamer Merlin and his prophecies,
> And of a dragon and a finless fish,
> A clip-winged griffin and a moulten raven,
> A crouching lion and a ramping cat,
> And such a deal of skimble-skamble stuff
> As puts me from my faith. I tell you what —
> He held me last night at least nine hours
> In reckoning up the several devils' names
> That were his lackeys. I cried, 'hum', and 'well, go to',
> But marked him not a word. O, he is as tedious
> As a tired horse, a railing wife,
> Worse than a smoky house — I had rather live
> With cheese and garlic in a windmill, far,
> Than feed on cates and have him talk to me
> In any summer house in Christendom.

Garlic was clearly regarded with some apprehension. In *A Midsummer Night's Dream*, Bottom advises his fellow players: 'And, most dear actors, eat no onions nor garlic, for we are to utter sweet breath.'

Spices, though, were highly valued. In *Henry V*, Orleans describes the Dauphin's horse: 'He's the colour of nutmeg.' And the Dauphin replies: 'And of the heat of the ginger. It is a beast for Perseus: he is pure air and fire ... he is indeed a horse; and all other jades you may call beasts.'

In *The Winter's Tale*, the Clown recounts an entire shopping list:

I cannot do't without counters. Let me see; what am I to buy for our sheep-shearing feast? Three pound of sugar, five pound of currants, rice — what will this sister of mine do with rice? But my father hath made her mistress of the feast and she lays it on ... I must have saffron to colour the warden pies; mace; dates? None, that's out of my note; nutmegs, seven; a race or two of ginger, but that I may beg; four pound of prunes, and as many of raisins o' the sun.

GOOSE AND OTHER MOVEABLE FEASTS

When Elizabeth I was brought the news of her navy's victory over the Spanish Armada, it was Michaelmas Day and she was eating roast goose – one of her favourite dishes. Overjoyed at the news, she decreed that it should be commemorated by eating goose every Michaelmas Day.

Goose was not the only dish Elizabeth enjoyed, and although she managed never to put on the weight her father did, she did spend a lot of time feasting. This was often as a guest of favoured members of the aristocracy as she made her 'progress' around the country, where extraordinary preparations would be made before her arrival. When she went to Stafford in 1575, the town repointed the houses, gravelled the streets and repaired the old town cross. Elizabeth was presented with a tall cup valued at £30 by the town bailiffs and, after many most sweet and gracious words to the great comfort of the poor inhabitants of Stafford she passed along through the market place, and so in at the Crabbery Lane to the Broad Eye and over at the new bridge where the bailiffs left her majesty, her highness going directly to Stafford Castle where she stayed to dinner and so parted thence.

The Queen's progress was a major undertaking and one she undertook every

Meat was the focal point of the feasts, aimed at showing the social status of the host. Boars' heads and stuffed swans were particularly impressive dishes.

British Beef

Venison was one of the favourite Tudor meats. Henry VIII prided himself on his prowess in the hunting field, but beef and mutton were also very popular and the quality of meat in Britain was generally thought to be particularly good, according to foreign visitors.

year until the end of the 1570s. She took most of her court with her, and between 200 and 300 carts of her own possessions and matters pertaining to her government. Accommodation and food had to be found for all, not just the courtly inner circle. She expected a proper welcome too. Stafford had fallen on hard times when she visited it, but Norwich pulled all the stops out during her 1578 progress with a welcoming pageant that included a boy dressed as Mercury riding in a coach decorated with birds and clouds. At the sound of a fanfare, he stepped out, delivered a speech of welcome to the Queen and then drove off in his carriage.

We do have a record of the feasts she enjoyed while staying with Robert Dudley, who became the first Earl of Leicester, over 19 days of her royal progress of 1575 – 10 oxen were consumed daily. Dudley was rumoured to be her lover and certainly had designs on becoming her husband. Another rumour suggests that he murdered his first wife to free himself so that Elizabeth could become his second.

FISH

Fishing became particularly important in Tudor times. Fish had always been vital because of the fasts imposed by the Church, when they were a substitute for meat, and during the times of year when meat was simply in short supply. Now, added to this demand, another practical consideration came to the fore.

Fishermen were vital in maintaining seamanship skills at a time when invasion was expected almost constantly, and England for the first time built up its navy.

The fish brought in from the sea included sole, flounder, cod, haddock, plaice, whiting and conger eel. Of course, the fish could not travel far from the coast without salting due to the unreliability of the roads and salted fish was often used in stews. Inland, freshwater fish were obtained from rivers, including salmon, perch, pike, trout, carp and eels. And there were numerous stewponds, specially constructed ponds in which the wealthy and the monasteries would keep their own freshwater fish, particularly carp.

Shellfish such as mussels, cockles and oysters were also popular and even made their way to the London markets.

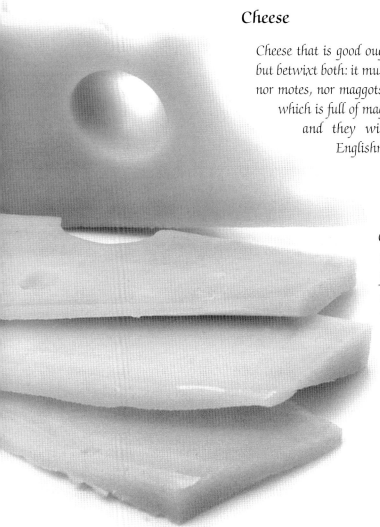

Cheese

Cheese that is good ought not to be too hard nor too soft, but betwixt both: it must be of good savour, not full of eyes, nor motes, nor maggots. Yet in High Germany the cheese which is full of maggots is called there the best cheese, and they will eat the maggots as fast as Englishmen do comfits.

From *Dietary of Health*, Andrew Boorde, 1547.

Cheese was very regional – an almost unimaginably wide variety could be found around Britain made either of cow or sheep milk and with a wide range of flavourings and colours.

Food and Furniture

Many of the dining room features we know today received their names around this time, and very often they were French inventions. A buffet, for instance, was originally the shelving on which the silver was displayed. Later, the food would be placed there too, giving the modern meaning of the word. The shelves or boards of the buffet would be known as 'cup boards' or 'dresses' (French for set up or laid, as in tables) and these later became cupboards and dressers. Sideboards were, of course, those 'bordes' (tables) set up at the side of the room where the food was placed before serving.

MANNERS AND MEALTIMES

In 1530, Erasmus wrote a treatise on manners *de civilitate morum puerilium* (On the Civility of the Behaviour of Boys). This didn't deal exclusively on table manners, but they certainly featured largely, and it was the beginning of documentary evidence on the importance of manners in society. Bodily functions became increasingly hidden, so when in company it began to be bad form to belch, snort, vomit, fart or spit. Gradually, people stopped using their hands and had their own cutlery and drinking vessels. It was all a sign of being civilised and, in the next century in France, etiquette would play such a prominent part at the court of Louis XIV that breaking the rules would provoke the monarch's displeasure. It was the beginning of 'good taste', in a sense that took it far beyond food.

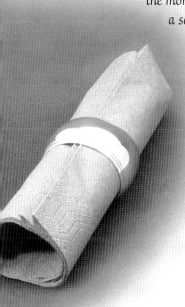

As in the preceding centuries, the main meal of the day in England, dinner, was taken around eleven o'clock in the morning. For the nobility it would certainly be the first meal of the day and for everyone it was the largest. It would take centuries for dinner to move back to the evening, to be replaced by a midday meal called lunch or luncheon.

It was towards the end of this period that napkins became not only extensively used but elaborately folded. Napkin folding became an art and at important dinners

they could assume the shapes of animals and birds or fruit. In the next century it even became a profession, and at Versailles they were transformed into frogs, boats and swans.

It was in the latter half of the Sixteenth Century, too, that forks started to make a more general appearance. There had been a few forks mentioned before this time, or early versions of them, but now they became much more accepted in royal and aristocratic circles, the fashion being led by Henri III of France. At first, beyond these elevated circles, they were regarded as rather effeminate and treated with derision, but from France, Italy and Spain the trend began to spread until by the early Seventeenth Century, they even reached England. Square wooden trenchers (in pewter or even silver-gilt for the very wealthy) were still in common use, but towards the end of this century, in Italy, they became circular and as this trend gradually spread across Europe, trenchers were transformed into what we now recognise as plates.

Italians in general and the Venetians in particular were notably accomplished when it came to the presentation of food. In 1581, Vincenzo Cervio wrote a book of advice for those carving meat and fowl. He disdained the concept of carving on a dish, preferring the more eye-catching method of holding the joint aloft on a carving fork and slicing pieces off it by means of the sharpest of knives so that they fell on a plate below to form a perfectly symmetrical pattern. All this plus you had to stand in such a way to show off your elegant figure in full view of your audience of diners while performing this extraordinary feat with the greatest rapidity. No wonder carvers were highly regarded.

THE WINE CELLAR

Not much water was drunk in Tudor times, mostly because it was so difficult to find fresh, clean water. Milk was drunk, but again not in great quantities as there was no way to keep it from souring. Most people drank ale and beer or (if they were rich) wine all day. The ale and beer were not as strong as they are today and were flavoured with pepper or berries. Nevertheless, one cannot help wondering if most of the population spent its time in a continual alcoholic haze, as consumption of these albeit comparatively weak alcoholic drinks were thought to have been around a gallon a day for every man, woman and child.

Tudor tastes in drink were similar to their tastes in food, so even though the wines tended to be sweet and heavy to start with, usually spices, such as cinnamon, ginger, nutmeg and cloves, together with sugar were added – rather like the mulled wine or gluhwein commonly served at Christmas. Wine arrived in casks and needed straining before serving to get rid of any undesirable extras. It was measured in tuns.

Tudor drinks

Rhenish – A strong German wine
Claret – French red wine from Gascony
Canary – A white wine from the Canary Islands

Wine and beer were the drinks of choice in an age when water was foul and diseased. The wine would be flavoured with spices such as cinnamon, ginger, nutmeg and cloves with sugar added, similar to mulled wine.

Sack – Spanish sherry (fortified wine)
Perry – Pear cider
Cider – Fermented drink made from apples
Mead – A sweet alcoholic drink made from honey and spices
Aqua vita – Bandy or other spirits
Hypocras – A sweet liqueur from the Eastern Mediterranean, very expensive
    and so only served at royal banquets
Beer – Brewed from hops
Ale – A fermented drink made from malt and water
Posset – A mixture of eggs, milk and ale

SUGAR AND SPICE

The poor continued to use honey as a sweetener, keeping their own black (not striped) bees in wicker or straw hives. English honey was regarded as being of particularly high quality, nevertheless, the Tudor period saw the relentless rise in popularity of sugar. Sugar had passed into the hands of the Crusaders and it had been established as a crop in Cyprus, Morocco, Madeira, the Azores and the Canaries.

Sugar had first been regarded as a medicine but increasingly became a favourite part of the diet. It came in large square or cone shaped lumps weighing over a kilogram, which had to be grated or pounded before they could be used. It remained expensive enough only to be available to the richest in the land and triggered the mania for puddings, pastries, biscuits and sweetmeats such as 'marchpane' or marzipan. It was graded as follows:

- Madeira sugar was the finest – white and easily absorbed in cooking

- Barbary or Canary sugar was slightly coarser

- The most common form of sugar was coarse and brown, but good for syrups and marinades

The Tudors loved spicy foods, though the spices they preferred tended to be sweet rather than hot. Accordingly, they classed certain dried fruits as spices and so, especially for feasts, would use liberal amounts of mace, cloves, cinnamon, ginger, pepper, caraway, currants, dates and raisins. However, spices were still extremely expensive and so, except by the very rich, they were only used for special occasions.

Another import that first appeared in the second half of the Sixteenth Century was tobacco. Having arrived from the New World, it was cultivated in Spain and by the newly arrived English settlers in Virginia. It was not only smoked in pipes, it could be chewed, or used as snuff or 'powdered tobacco' when it could be mixed with other precious ingredients, such as musk, amber and bergamot – this became fashionable over time with ladies too. There followed numerous attempts at the prohibition of tobacco growing – in England in 1604, the Ottoman Empire in 1611, Sweden and Denmark in 1632, Naples in 1637 and China in 1642 – but all to no avail. By the end of the next century, it would be more popular even than tea and coffee.

Fruit

Fresh fruit was still regarded as unsafe in Tudor times and was believed to carry disease if eaten raw. During the plague of 1569, the selling of fresh fruit was banned by law. Nevertheless, quantities of it were grown including apples, pears, cherries, damsons, plums, strawberries and gooseberries. They were, however, cooked either in puddings or as a part of a meat dish.

Food as Medicine

Many kinds of food – not just herbs – were regarded in Tudor times as a form of medicine. Much of this thinking originated in the writings of Hippocrates in ancient Greece (c.460–377BC) and was based on a theory of four humours. These were bile, blood, choler and melancholy, and the understanding of them was common coinage. They recur frequently, for instance, in Shakespeare's plays. Malvolio was the ultimate melancholic man, while Hotspur was a choleric one. The same characteristics were ascribed to different foods, drinks and spices and so when someone became ill, it was believed to be because their humours were out of balance. The remedy, clearly, would be to give food and drink of the right humours to restore the balance.

TUDOR NOVELTIES

The Tudors loved novelty whether in entertainment, dress or food, and this period introduced a huge number of previously unknown delicacies to their tables. Sugar, as we have already seen, made great inroads into Sixteenth Century cookery. Explorations to the New World introduced the tomato (or love apple) from Mexico, the potato from Chile and the kidney bean from Peru, and such exotica as pineapples (only for the wealthiest in the land and later used as a symbol for dukedoms), turkeys and vanilla.

One of the greatest novelties in Tudor times came in the form of hot drinks – a previously unknown phenomenon. Now three versions of this concept arrived all at once. Two came from the New World, coffee and chocolate, and the third, tea, came from the East. As with many new foods, at first they were regarded mostly as medicines, believed to work best as stimulants, especially for

those who were working long hours. Tea was
thought to contribute to a long and healthy life,
as demonstrated in the Chinese people who
drank so much of it.

Some innovations came from less far afield. The
Dutch had developed new agricultural techniques
and with them new crops – such as the orange carrot we
are familiar with today – and these were eagerly adopted. Landowners began to
read the practical agricultural advice of the classical authors in their attempts
to improve farming yields and methods. 'Whosoever does not maintain the
Plough, destroys this Kingdom', thundered Robert Cecil in the House of
Commons in 1601.

TUDOR COOKBOOK

It was during the Tudor period that, for the first time, cookery books were
printed. They bore little resemblance to the cookery books of today but, unlike
the earlier Medieval handwritten recipes, the Tudor versions began to include
quantities in terms of spoonfuls, dishes and ladlefuls, timings (though given the
nature of cooking fires these could only be approximate) and other practical
advice. Copies of some of these first cookbooks still survive in the British
Library. *A Proper New Booke of Cookery*, for instance, was published
anonymously in 1575 and contains recipes for broths, roast meats, pies and
preserves. Its fruit and flower tarts are particularly evocative – there is one for
damsons with borage flowers and one of 'Marygoldes, prim roses and cowslips'.
The Widdowes Treasure was written by John Partridge and published in 1595.
As well as recipes for the table, he also gives advice on medical matters or
'Sundry precious and approved secrets in Phisicke and Chirurgery, for the health
and pleasure of mankind'. These include everything from how to cure chapped
lips to stimulating the growth of your beard. *The Good Huswifes Jewell* was
written by Thomas Dawson and published in 1585. He went on to write *The
Good Huswifes Handmaid for the kitchen* in 1594 and *The Book of Carving
and Sewing* in 1597, covering between the three everything from animal
husbandry to needlework to managing your servants – and of course the recipes
themselves. He was probably the first writer to give quantities in pounds and
ounces, pints and gallons.

Italian Pudding

The marrow of the original recipe has been left out of this version because of availability, and the amount of butter has been reduced to make it slightly healthier (so it requires more milk)

225g / 8oz bread
$1/3$ cup sugar, plus 1 tbsp for sprinkling
225g / 8oz raisins
$1/2$ cup butter, melted
2 cups milk
4 eggs
$3/4$ tsp nutmeg
2 tbsp rosewater
Dates, destoned (for garnish)

Remove the crusts from the bread. Cut it into $2^1/2$cm / 1in cubes. Mix the sugar with the raisins and combine with the bread cubes, making sure the raisins are distributed evenly. Place the bread mixture in a casserole dish. In a separate bowl, mix the butter, milk, eggs, nutmeg and rosewater. Pour carefully over the bread cubes. Garnish with sliced dates. Cover and bake in a 170ºC / 325ºF / gas mark 3 oven for 45 minutes or until a knife inserted in the centre comes out clean. Sprinkle with a coarse-grained sugar and bake uncovered for 15 more minutes. Serve hot.

Source: *A new booke of Cookerie*: To make an Italian Pudding. Take a Penny white Loafe, pare off the crust, and cut it in square pieces like vnto great Dyes, mince a pound of Beefe Suit small: take halfe a pound of Razins of the Sunne, stone them and mingle them together, and season them with Sugar, Rosewater, and Nutmegge, wet these things in foure Egges, and stirre them very tenderly for breaking the Bread: then put it into a Dish, and pricke three or foure pieces of Marrow, and some sliced Dates: put it into an Ouen hot enough for a Chewet: if your Ouen be too hot, it will burne: if too colde, it will be heauy: when it is bakte scrape on Sugar, and serue it hot at dinner, but not at Supper.

A Dish of Artichokes

$^1\!/_2$ tsp pepper
$^1\!/_2$ tsp cinnamon
$^1\!/_2$ tsp ginger
2 tbsp water
10–12 artichoke bottoms, cooked
4 tbsp butter
Dash of vinegar
1 tbsp large crystal sugar

Mix the pepper, cinnamon, and ginger with water. Bring to a boil and remove from the heat. Add the artichoke bottoms and allow to marinate for 15 minutes. Place into a baking dish and add the butter and vinegar. Bake at 180°C / 350°F / gas mark 4 for 15 minutes. Sprinkle with sugar and serve.

Source: *The Good Huswifes Jewell*, T. Dawson: To make a dishe of Artechokes. Take your Artechokes and pare away all the top even to the meate and boyle them in sweete broth till they be somewhat tender, then take them out, and put them into a dishe, and seethe them with Pepper, synamon and ginger, and then put in your dishe that you meane to bake them in, and put in Marrowe to them good store, and so let them bake, and when they be baked, put in a little Vinegar and butter, and sticke three or foure leaves of the Artechoks in the dishe when you serve them up, and scrape Suger on the dish.

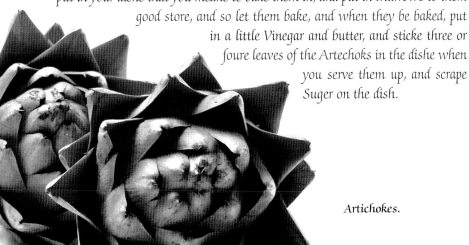

Artichokes.

Gooseberry Fool

Although the recipe does not give a quantity, a good amount of sugar would be needed for this recipe to counteract the sourness of the fruit – especially given the sweetness of the Tudor tooth

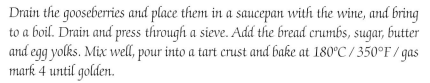

    2 tins / 425g / 15oz gooseberries
    1 cup wine
    1 slice bread, ground into crumbs
    $^1/_2$ cup sugar
    2 tbsp butter, melted
    6 egg yolks

Drain the gooseberries and place them in a saucepan with the wine, and bring to a boil. Drain and press through a sieve. Add the bread crumbs, sugar, butter and egg yolks. Mix well, pour into a tart crust and bake at 180°C / 350°F / gas mark 4 until golden.

Source: *A Proper Newe Booke of Cokerye*, Anne Ahmed (ed.): To make a tarte of goseberies. Take goseberies and parboyle them in whyte wyne, claret, or ale, and boyle with all a lyttle whyte breade, then take them up and drawe them throughe a strayner as thycke as you can with the yolckes of syxe egges, then season it up with suger, halfe a dysshe of butter, so bake it.

Diverse Salads

The notes for this recipe state that it can be used for a diverse range of vegetables – here, it is based on cauliflower. Like many other recipes of the time, this one uses sugar and what we would now call 'sweet spices' in a way that is a bit surprising to the modern palate

    1 head of cauliflower
    2 tbsp currants
    3 tbsp butter
    1 tsp sugar
    $^1/_4$ tsp cinnamon
    $^1/_4$ tsp ginger
    Dash of vinegar
    1 egg, hard boiled

Cut up the cauliflower and parboil until just tender, adding currants halfway through. Drain and set aside. Melt the butter in a large saucepan. Mix in the cauliflower and add the sugar, spices and vinegar. Cut the egg into quarters and use as a garnish. Serve hot.

Source: *A new booke of Cookerie*, J. Murrell: *Diuers Sallets boyled. Parboyle Spinage, and chop it fine, with the edges of two hard Trenchers vpon a boord, or the backe of two chopping Kniues: then set them on a Chafingdish of coales with Butter and Uinegar. Season it with Sinamon, Ginger, Sugar, and a few parboyld Currins. Then cut hard Egges into quarters to garnish it withall, and serue it vpon sippets. So may you serue Burrage, Buglosse, Endiffe, Suckory, Coleflowers, Sorrel, Marigold leaues, water Cresses, Leekes boyled, Onions, Sparragus, Rocket, Alexanders. Parboyle them, and season them all alike: whether it be with Oyle and Uinegar, or Butter and Uinegar, Sinamon, Ginger, Sugar, and Butter: Egges are necessary, or at least very good for all boyld Sallets.*

Meat Pies

The extra marrow or lard in the original recipe is not absolutely necessary due to the fat content in most commercially available meats. If you're using minced beef or mutton with very little fat then you'll need to add a tablespoon or two of lard

Filling:
675g / 1^1/$_2$lb mutton or beef, minced
55g / 2oz prunes, chopped
55g / 2oz dates, chopped
55g / 2oz raisins
2 tbsp vinegar
^{1}/$_2$ tsp pepper
^{1}/$_2$ tsp salt
Pinch of saffron, ground

Crust:
115g / 4oz lard
225g / 8oz flour
Pinch of salt
1 dsp water
1 egg yolk, beaten

Mix the filling ingredients and set aside. Rub the lard into the flour with a pinch of salt until the mixture resembles fine bread crumbs. Add a little cold water and the beaten egg, mix. Leave to rest for 30 minutes. Separate into eight portions and roll out on a floured pastry board. Place one eighth of the filling into each, fold over, and seal with water. Place in a dish and bake at 180°C / 350°F / gas mark 4 until the crust is golden – about 30 minutes.

Source: *A Proper Newe Booke of Cokerye*, Anne Ahmed (ed.): To make Pyes. Pyes of mutton or beif must be fyne mynced and ceasoned wyth pepper and salte, and a lyttle saffron to coloure it, suet or marrow a good quantite, a lyttle vyneger, prumes, greate raysins, and dates, take the fattest of the broathe of powdred beyfe, and yf you wyll haue paest royall, take butter and yolkes of egges, and to tempre the flowre to make the paeste.

Stuffed Cabbage
This recipe uses the sweet spice mixture, powder douce, which was also popular in the Medieval period

    1 small red cabbage
    450g / 1lb ground pork
    3 eggs
    2 tbsp powder douce (see page 57)

Place the cabbage whole into boiling water and cook until the leaves can be peeled back without breaking – about 30 minutes. Remove from the water, carefully open the outer leaves and cut out the centre. Mix the remaining ingredients together and use them to fill the cabbage, securing the leaves with toothpicks. Bake at 190°C / 375°F / gas mark 5 for 50 minutes, or until cooked through. Pull back the leaves and cut the filling into cubes to serve.

Source: *Ouverture de Cuisine*, D. Myers (trans.): To make a stuffed cabbage. Take a red cabbage that is not too large, & put it to boil whole sweetly, & leave it so a long time that you can open the leaves the one behind the other, while the leaves of the cabbage are large like a fist, cut that out, & put chopped meat therein that it will be arrayed like the other meats with eggs & spices, & then layer the cabbage with the leaves all around, that it will be well bound, & put it to cook, sausages with, or that which you want.

CEREAL DIFFERENCES

It is fascinating to note that Europeans were alone in eating so much meat and protein during this – and many other – periods. Other cultures had over centuries developed quite different diets based mostly on grains and vegetables. This was not just the case in the rice-based East but also in Africa and pre-Columbian America. Part of the reason why the rich of Europe were able to continue feasting on meat was that there were vast tracts of empty land that could be used for grazing. In addition, the population was at this point relatively small, the meat-eating class even smaller. In more densely populated regions, such as the East, land could not be spared to raise cattle and was devoted instead to rice. One Seventeenth Century traveller to the island of Sumatra observed:

> One has to be a very great lord in Sumatra to have a boiled or roast chicken, which moreover has to last for the whole day. Therefore they say that two thousand Christians on their island would soon exhaust the supply of cattle and poultry.

Rice was also known in Europe, though it was by no means as popular a grain as wheat, oats or barley. From the Fifteenth Century, it was grown in Italy, but it was not much appreciated and, over the next few centuries, it would generally be reserved for use as a form of emergency rations during famines.

In Europe, the king of grains was wheat – the basis of that necessity of daily bread. Oats were grown principally as fodder for horses (though especially in northern parts, oats were part of the human diet too, in the form of porridge). The all-important wheat harvest came, however, with an added problem. You cannot successfully grow it on the same land two years running as it so depletes the earth. This was the reason that, for centuries before the Tudors, crops were rotated, usually in a three-year pattern. Any given field would produce wheat one year, another crop the next and lie fallow for a third.

The Seventeenth Century:
Throughout the century during Winter the Thames freezes over and the 'Frost Fair' takes place on the frosen river.

1642-49: Civil War in England; Charles I is beheaded by Cromwell.

1665: The Great Plague of London.

1666: The Great Fire of London.

Chapter 5

The
Seventeenth Century

T HE SEVENTEENTH Century was a period that suffered repeated turbulent change. It began with the last years of the Elizabethan era, *Gloriana*, a period almost mythologised for its peace and prosperity, but it was to see the execution of a king, bloody civil war, plague and fire. A new class of landowners – created as a result of Henry VIII's dissolution of the monasteries and nothing to do with the old powerful families of court – came into its own and created a new political dynamic. Morals, in the meantime, yo-yoed from court debauchery to the strictest Puritanism and back again.

Against such a background, it is astonishing that agriculture, the improvement of diet, and culinary expertise managed to survive as well as they did. In fact, they not only survived but thrived and were to change radically over the period. Tastes changed, too. The longstanding preference for sweet and spicy foods was gradually overturned during the Seventeenth Century, so by the end of the period the fashion was for the salty, savoury flavours for meat, fish and other main courses that have persisted to this day. Not that sugar was left out in the cold. This century saw its use become increasingly widespread and

sweetmeats of all kinds became very popular.

Books of 'receipts' or recipes flourished. Some, such as Sarah Longe's *Receipt Booke* of 1610 were in manuscript form and covered recipes not just for general 'Cokery' but also for 'preserves and conserves' (that sweet tooth was definitely growing) and 'Physicke and Chirurgery' – health still being generally regarded as under the domain of the kitchen.

As the century wore on, there was something of a flurry of cookery book publishing that reached its height, rather surprisingly, during the Commonwealth, the rule of the Puritans under the guidance of Oliver Cromwell in the 1650s. It seems ironic that during a period that saw the abolition of the monarchy, the closure of the theatres and when even the Christmas feast was regarded as ungodly, books such as *The Queens Closet Opened* should have been such a huge success. First published in 1655, it had ten new editions brought out before the end of the century and its popularity was certainly helped by a nostalgic yearning for the ways of the old aristocracy, and the secrets of their extravagant and glittering lives.

The Queens Closet Opened was written by the mysterious 'W. M.', who clearly understood this particular Zeitgeist. On the title page, the author explains that the book's recipes came from the kitchens of no less a personage than Henrietta Maria, wife of King Charles I. He goes on to reveal 'incomparable Secrets in Physick, Chirurgery, Preserving and Candying etc which were presented unto the Queen by the most Experienced Persons of the Times, many whereof were had in esteem when She pleased to descend to private recreations.' The book, as W. M. has promised, covers recipes in 'The Compleat Cook', confectionery in 'A Queen's Delight' and remedies in 'The Pearl of Practice'. Naturally, many of the recipes within all three chapters contained ingredients that were so exotic or expensive they were far beyond the reach of the average cook – but perhaps that added to the wow factor.

'The Accomplisht Cook' was written by Robert May and published in 1660, the year of the restoration of the monarchy, when he was 72 years old and had spent a lifetime as a chef. In much the same vein as *The Queens Closet Opened*, he boasts that his recipes 'were formerly the delights of the Nobility, before good housekeeping had left England'. May pulls out all the stops with recipes for the flamboyant school of dining featuring such centrepieces as a pastry stag filled with claret to resemble blood – the thrill of the chase brought to the table – a tortoise stewed with eggs, and a pie filled with live frogs and birds that would

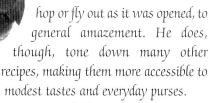

hop or fly out as it was opened, to general amazement. He does, though, tone down many other recipes, making them more accessible to modest tastes and everyday purses.

May had spent time in Paris learning his trade and he included in *The Accomplisht Cook* recipes not just from France, but also from Spain, Italy, Turkey and Persia. He had spotted a trend that was to become a major influence in the English kitchen. Foreign recipes – especially from France – were to transform English tastes. In the meantime, a great change in cooking was taking place throughout Europe.

Francois Pierre de La Varenne had published his cookery book, *The French Cook*, in 1650 and it was to transform English and French cooking. Modern preparations such as delicate flour-based (roux) sauces replaced the more robust traditional cooking methods. Sweet, reduced sauces (coulis) based on fruit were introduced, as were more of those increasingly popular salty tastes in the form of anchovies and capers.

While the English took all of this up with alacrity, they also retained roasting as a favoured method of cooking meat. In 1664, Hannah Woolley published her second book, *The Cook's Guide: or Rare receipts for cookery*, which not only gave traditional recipes and cooking methods, but advice on serving and etiquette. She wrote several others and managed to establish herself as that rare phenomenon, a lady author in the Seventeenth Century. In fact, women were behind most of the recipes that appeared in the cookbooks, even if their authors were men. Gervase Markham, for instance, admits in his *Countrey Contentments* that his recipes were the work of an 'honourable countess'. In a time when only one in ten women could read – and even they were often not taught to write – perhaps the predominance of male cookery writers is not surprising.

The other theory often put forward for the avalanche of Seventeenth Century cookbooks is that many of the chefs who had worked for the monarchy and aristocracy were left jobless, as their masters fled abroad (those who were lucky enough to escape with their lives). It must have seemed an obvious task to turn their hands to.

While there were many novelties appearing on the table, meat (beef, mutton, pork) was still the most popular food for those who could afford it. Venison was, of course, still highly regarded and widely served. 'We had at dinner a couple of venison pasties,' complained Samuel Pepys, 'of which I ate but little, being almost cloyed having been at five pasties in three days.' Pepys elsewhere mentions his love of the newly arrived turkey as well as partridge, pheasant, duck and goose.

LONDON'S MARKETS

During the course of the century, improvements went on apace in the agricultural world but, as the towns and cities were growing, it became increasingly important to move the produce of the countryside to the burgeoning urban population. At the beginning of the century there were already 800 markets around England and in London there were 16 major markets specialising in particular foodstuffs. Leadenhall sold corn and meat as well as hops from Kent. Meat was available at Smithfields or the Shambles in St Nicholas Street. Poultry was sold at Stocks Market (on the site of the present Mansion House). New Fish Street and Billingsgate provided the capital with cheap shellfish (even lobster was not too expensive), as well as cod, trout, salmon, eels, crab, carp and anchovies but also salt, grain, onions and imported oranges. Covent Garden was just starting up, selling fruit and vegetables.

Many foodstuffs were, though, sold by hawkers crying their wares through the streets. Such wares included fish, meat and imported fruit – most famously sold by Nell Gwyn, the orange girl at the Theatre Royal who was to become the mistress of Charles II. In spite of Nell's popularity, fresh fruit was still somewhat distrusted. Samuel Pepys, whose diary gives a unique insight into life in the London of the second half of the Seventeenth Century, believed it was bad for the stomach. Potatoes were rarely eaten, being a possible cause of flatulence and leprosy. Tomatoes, too, were unpopular as they were thought to cause gout and cancer. Pepys was persuaded, albeit unwillingly, to drink orange juice. He reported:

> I drank a glass of a pint, I believe, at one draught, of the juice of oranges
> of whose peel they make comfits; and here they drink the juice as wine,
> with sugar, and it is very fine drink; but it being new [fresh] I was

doubtful whether it might not do me hurt.

Pepys was a gourmand and recorded his dinner parties with gusto. In 1663 he gave a 'great dinner':

> We had a fricassee of rabbits and chicken, a leg of mutton boiled, three carps in a dish, a great dish of a side of lamb, a dish of roasted pigeons, a dish of four lobsters, three tarts, a lamprey pie … a dish of anchovies, good wine of several sorts.

He was, like most of his contemporaries, a great drinker of wine and beer, wine being imported at the time from France, Spain, the Canaries and Germany. He eschewed water, believing it to be bad for the health and in this he was probably right given that it often came from polluted rivers. Beer was available everywhere (the official allowance for a sailor was eight pints a day) and was cheap, though not as cheap as ale. Beer, wine and ale were often warmed and spiced before drinking. The poorest, however, were soon to turn to the iniquitous cheap gin, to be immortalised in Hogarth's moral engravings of the next century, 'Gin Lane', the dissolute inhabitants of which stood in stark contrast to the more wholesome inhabitants of his other set of engravings, 'Beer Lane'.

In the Seventeenth Century, however, the alehouse was not commonly regarded as a good influence. Richard Gough wrote his fascinating gossip about his neighbours, *The History of Myddle* around 1700 reflecting back on the previous 50 years and describing each of them according to the place they sat in church. However, much of their time was spent elsewhere and stories of drunkenness and the alehouse abound, such as the one concerning the nephew of the Rector of Myddle:

> This William Crosse had a good estate in lands and a fair house in Yorton. He married Judith, the daughter of Mr Francis Whitcombe of Berwicke. But that which sowered all, was that this William Crosse and his wife were both overmuch addicted to drunkenness, and it is no marvel that they consumed the marriage portion (which was considerable), in a short time, and afterwards the lands. When William Crosse had sold his lands in Yorton he came to Billmarsh, where he followed the same way of drinking as before, for he and his wife went daily to the alehouse and soon after the cows went thither also; and when his stock was spent he sold his lease to Nathaniel Reve, and removed to Shrewsbury, where he took a little house on the rack rent, and there followed the same way of drinking.

He died soon after he went to Shrewsbury, and as his life was extravagant, so his end was strange, for as he sat in an alehouse cellar upon the stand that holds the barrels, and whilst another was drawing drink by him, he was taken with an apoplexy, and fell down dead. The other man thought he was playing the wag and said, arise, why dost thou play the fool? – but when the other man went to him he found that he was dead, and called the neighbours, but he could not be recovered.

For the very rich even beyond the capital, indulgence was rarely called to such account. On a visit to Cambridge, the Earl of Bedford stayed at the Red Lion Inn and the following bill remains:

	£	s	d
For a large pike with all sorts of fish about it	2	18	6
For a surloin of beef		13	0
For making a pasty		12	0
For a shoulder, neck and a breast of mutton		7	0
For a couple of geese		8	0
For a dish of capons and sausages		9	0
For a ham, eight chickens and cauliflowers	1	10	0
For a dish of collared pig		11	0
For a frigize [fricassee] of rabbits and chickens		5	0
For salading		1	6
For a dish of mince pies		8	6
Second course			
For 2 dishes of all sorts of wild fowl	1	15	6
For a brace of pheasants		7	6
For a brace of curlews and partridge		5	0
For a dish of fat chickens and pigeons		8	6
For a stand of pickles and collared eels		17	0
For a large jowl of sturgeon	1	15	0
For a dish of tarts with ladies tarts		11	6
For a dish of fruit		3	6
For lemons and double refined sugar		3	6
For oil and vinegar		2	5

Later that day he ordered supper at the same hostelry.

Chocolate and Coffee

Chocolate and coffee had made their first appearance in the previous century, but now they became all the rage. The first coffee house was opened in London in 1652 by Pasqua Rosee, the servant of a Turkish merchant. More coffee houses appeared in all the major towns and became both social meeting places and hotbeds of political discussion.

This was the heyday of the political pamphlet or petition – they could be easily published and distributed on the street – and while many were on serious political issues, others focused on more everyday matters. One such defends the coffee house as the 'Citizens' Academy' where coffee 'both keeps us sober and can make us so'. This was, in fact, written in answer to a previous pamphlet decrying the coffee house, entitled 'The Women's Petition against Coffee' that claimed that men 'like so many frogs in a puddle … sup muddy water and murmur insignificant notes till half a dozen of them out-babble an equal number of us at gossiping.'

Both chocolate and coffee were regarded as stimulants (as indeed they are known to be today) and so beneficial for those who were at their books until late into the night. According to William Coles in 1657, however, in *Adam in Eden* chocolate had other properties:

> The Confection made of Cacao called Chocolate or Chocoletto, which may be had … in London at reasonable rates, is of wonderful efficacy for the procreation of children: for it not only vehemently incites to Venus, but causeth Conception in women … and besides that it preserves health, for it makes such as take it often to become fat and corpulent, fair and amiable.

THE NEW FARMING

It was not only in the cooking or importing of food that England saw changes. Many gentlemen began to take a greater interest in their agricultural lands and farming methods. New improved ploughs, planting and cultivation techniques all brought benefits. They looked to older strategies too, studying the classics for their practices and at the same time read the contemporary cultivation guides by writers like William Lawson, who advised on fruit and vegetable growing and beekeeping, or Nicolas de Bonnefons, author of *The French gardiner,* instructing how to cultivate all sorts of fruit trees.

Accordingly, increasing numbers of apples, pears, strawberries, cucumbers, melons and cherries were planted and, for the first time, the English dared to eat fresh fruit raw as well as making it into jam or cooking it, or using it as a medical distillation. Naturally there was much advice on how and when to pick and eat it. *Lake's Almanack* of 1628 opined: 'If you would have fruits to keep long, then let them not be over-ripe on the tree and gather them about the first or last quarter of the moon.' Tradition has it that rain on St Swithin's Day (15 July) 'blesses and christens' apples, so they ripen. It was therefore best not to pick or eat them before then.

As for cooking fruit, there was plenty of advice there, too. Thomas Jenner in his book of 1653, *A Book of Fruits and Flowers,* says:

> To preserve Damsons. Take Damsons before they be full ripe, but gathered off the Tree. Allow to every pound of them a pound of Sugar, put a little Rose-water to them, and set them in the bottom of your pan one by one. Boil them with a soft fire, and as they seeth strew your Sugar upon them, and let them boil till the Syrup be thick. Then while the Syrup is yet warm, take the Damsons out and put them into a covered gally pot, Syrup and all.

Fresh fruit may have finally found its way into the diet, but it still carried with it certain dangers. According to Nicholas Culpeper in *The Compleat Herbal,* of 1653:

> All Plums are under Venus, and are like women, some better and some worse. As there is a great

diversity of kinds, so there is in the operation of Plums, for some that are sweet moisten the stomach, and make the belly soluble: those that are sour quench thirst more, and behind the belly. The moist and waterish do sooner corrupt in the stomach, but the firm do nourish more, and offend less.

DINING ON THE GRAND SCALE

Except for the period of the Puritan Commonwealth, at court and in other wealthy households, formal dinners became ever more extravagant. Waiting and kitchen staff created spectacular fantasies made out of food, there was music and entertainment and, as well as the fortunate diners, there were spectators who came to watch the show and finish off the leftovers – which were often considerable – when the nobility had taken their fill and retired. By this time, the food would be quite cold. Given the distances dishes usually had to travel from kitchen to table, even the original diners could only expect to eat, at best, luke warm meals.

Cutlery had now become established, especially at court. It was much easier to use knives and forks, as plates – either of silver, pewter or, later, china – became more widely available, given that a hard surface is needed to cut the food using implements. Manners became ever more refined. Hannah Woolley told her readers: 'Put not your Knife to your mouth unless it be to eat an Egge.' There were books written with the purpose of instructing servants on the proper way to carve meat, how to present food to the diner and the correct order of serving dishes. The servants were also still providing guests with a basin and ewer to wash their hands between courses – though of course, any manual handling of the food was frowned upon in polite circles. The sweet foods that ended the formal meal used quantities of sugar and would be served in beautiful dishes often made of silver. Sugar was believed by some to be an aphrodisiac.

One of the new foods that was introduced from the New World and that would have challenged the peacock for pride of place at banquets was the turkey. Now raised in East Anglia, they would walk to London in flocks of several hundred at a time, to be fattened up at the end before being sold. Across the Channel too, the rarest dishes carried the greatest prestige. The ortolan – a Cypriot bird found mostly in vineyards – became all the rage in France towards the end of the century. At the Princess of Conti's wedding in 1680, 16,000 livres were spent on these birds alone. Hazel grouse, green oysters, pineapples; anything unusual was immediately prized, almost regardless of what it would actually taste like. Huge quantities of these delicacies were ordered by the rich and huge quantities were left over, eaten by servants and finally sold to food dealers who would sell them on to the poor.

THE FRENCH TABLE

In *Les Délices de la campagne* (The Delights of the Countryside) by Nicolas de Bonnefons, published in 1654, the author outlines the way to lay a table for 30 people. Fourteen are placed along each side of a rectangular table, with one person at the 'top end' and another at the bottom, each 'the space of a chair apart'. 'The tablecloth must reach to the ground on all sides. There will be several salt cellars and table mats in the centre.' The meal will consist of eight courses, the last being composed of 'dry or liquid jams, crystallised sweets, musk pastilles, sugared almonds from Verdun, musky and amber-scented sugar.' The plates would be changed with every course, the napkins every two courses. Every guest would have a spoon, knife and possibly a fork, though not a glass. This was often brought by a servant, already filled, when called for, though in Germany it was already the custom that the glass remained by the diner's plate and was automatically filled by the servant when required. The fork was still not in general use even in the greatest dining rooms. Louis XIV enjoyed eating with his fingers. However, there was a growing awareness of manners. Young officers in Alsace, invited to the table of an archduke, were issued with a series of orders. They were to appear in a clean uniform and sober, and remain that way by not drinking after every mouthful. Furthermore, they were to wipe clean moustache and mouth before drinking, they were not to lick their fingers, spit in the plate nor wipe their noses on the tablecloth.

French cheeses were already long-established, both in the countryside where they were made and in the towns and cities to which they were carried. Fondues were cooked as well as cheese on toast or *croque monsieur*, while unsuccessful attempts were made to replicate Parmesan. It is thought that French peasants made fortunes by carrying cheese to the armies fighting in Italy and Germany in 1698. In some rural parts of France cheese was a major part of the diet of the poor, but it was not the only dairy product in widespread use. Milk was widely drunk (though frequently and secretly watered down by the supplier). Butter too was immensely important, principally as a major ingredient (along with such flavourings as amber, pepper, spices and rosewater, or all of them mixed together) in the rich sauces enjoyed by the wealthy. In this, France was unique. Her neighbours to the North used lard and bacon fat. To the South, they used olive oil, believing butter to be a cause of leprosy.

SEVENTEENTH CENTURY COOKBOOKS

Much survives from the 'closets' and 'receipt books' that belonged to the great houses of the Seventeenth Century as well as from published cookery books. The recipes were as likely to be about medicinal concoctions as they were about dishes to be served at dinner – and they included more general household advice. The Countess of Kent's *Choice Manual* advised:

> To take away a hoarseness. Take a turnip, cut a hole in the top of it, and fill it up with brown sugar-candy, and so roast it in the embers and eat it with butter. To take away the head-ache. Take the best salad oil and the glass half full with the tops of poppy flowers which groweth in the corn, set this in the sun a fortnight, and so keep it all the year, and anoint the temples of your head with it.

Robert May, in *The Accomplisht Cook* suggests a pastry dish that is to be seen rather than eaten at great feasts:

> Make the likeness of a Ship in Paste-board with Flags and Streamers, the Guns belonging to it of Kickses [kickshaws], bind them about with packthread, and cover them with close paste proportionable to the fashion of a Cannon with Carriages, lay them in places convenient as you see them in Ships of war, with such holes and trains of powder that they may all take fire; Place your Ship firm in the great Charger, then make a salt round about it and stick therein eggshells full of sweet water, you may by a great Pin take all the meat out of the egg by blowing and then fill it up with the rose-water, then in another Charger have the proportion of a Stag made of coarse paste, with a broad Arrow in the side of him, and his body filled up with claret-wine; in another Charger at the end have the proportion of a Castle with Battlements, Portcullises, Gates and Draw-Bridges made of Paste-board, the Guns and Kickses, and covered with coarse paste as the former; place it at a distance form the ship to fire at each other. The Stag being placed betwixt them with egg shells full of sweet water placed in salt.
>
> At each side of the Charger wherein is the Stag, place a Pie made of coarse paste filled with bran, and yellowed over with saffron or the yolks of eggs, gild them over in spots, as also the Stag, the Ship and the Castle;

bake them, and place them with gilt bay-leaves on turrets and tunnels of the Castle and Pies; being baked, make a hole in the bottom of your pies, take out the bran, put in your Frogs, and Birds and close up the holes with the same coarse paste, then cut the Lids nearly up; To be taken off the Tunnels, being all placed in order upon the Table, before you fire the trains of powder, order it so that some of the Ladies may be persuaded to pluck the Arrow out of the Stag, then will the Claret-wine follow, as blood that runneth out of a wound.

This being done with admiration to the beholders, after some short pause, fire the train of the Castle, that the pieces all of one side may go off, then fire the Trains of one side of the Ship as in a battle; next turn the chargers; and by degrees fire the trains of each side as before. This done, to sweeten the stink of the powder, let the Ladies take the egg shells full of sweet-waters and throw them at each other. All dangers being seemingly over, by this time you may suppose they will desire to see what is in the pies; where lifting first the lid off one pie, out skip some Frogs; which make the ladies to skip and shriek; next after the other pie, whence out come the birds, who by a natural instinct flying in the light, will put out the Candles, so that what with the flying Birds and skipping Frogs, the one above, the other beneath, will cause much delight and pleasure to the whole company: at length the Candles are lighted, and a banquet brought in, the Music sounds, and everyone with much delight and content rehearses their actions in the former passages. These were formerly the delights of the Nobility, before good housekeeping had left England and the Sword really acted that which was only counterfeited in such honest and laudable exercises as these.

Flowers

In the Seventeenth Century, as in the previous one, flowers were regarded as edible. They would still be eaten in savoury dishes, but now, with the increased availability of sugar, they would also be used in candied form for the 'banquet' or sweetmeat course that came at the end of a fine dinner:

> To candy all kind of flowers as they grow, with their stalks on. Take the Flowers and cut the stalk somewhat short: then take one pound of the whitest and hardest Sugar, put to it eight spoons of Rosewater, and boil it till it will roll between your finger and your thumb. Then take it from the fire and as it waxeth cold dip in all your Flowers: and taking them out suddenly, lay them one by one in the bottom of a sieve. Then turn a stool with the feet upwards, set the sieve on the feet, cover it with a fair linen cloth, and set a chafing-dish of coals in the midst of the stool and underneath the sieve: the heat thereof will dry your Candy presently. Then box them up, and they will keep all the year, and look very pleasantly.

> From *A Book of Fruits and Flowers*, Thomas Jenner, 1653.

Pancakes

> To make fine pancakes fried without butter or lard. Take a pint of cream and six new-laid eggs, beat them very well together, put in a quarter of a pound of sugar and one nutmeg grated or a little mace (which you please) and so much flour as will thicken as much as ordinary Pancake batter. Your pan must be heated reasonable hot and wiped with a clean cloth: this, done put in the batter as thick or thin as you please.

> From *The Compleat Cook*, 1671.

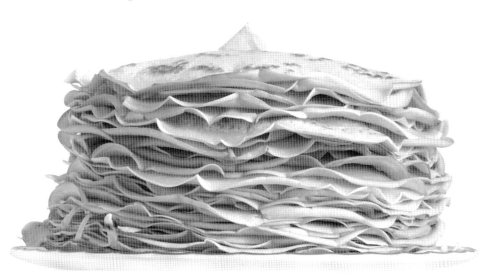

The Compleat Cook of 1671 had a pancake recipe calling for nutmeg or its covering skin, mace.

Cheese

> If you will have a very dainty Nettle Cheese, which is the finest Summer
> Cheese which can be eaten … as soon as it is drained from the brine, you
> shall lay it upon fresh Nettles, and cover it all over with the same, and let
> it ripen therein. Observing to renew your Nettles once in two days, and
> every time you renew them, to turn the Cheese. Gather your Nettles as
> much without stalks as may be, and make the bed both under and aloft as
> smooth as may be: for the fewer wrinkles your Cheese hath, the more
> dainty is your House-wife accounted.
>
> From the *English Housewife,* 1683.

Watercress

In the Twenty-first Century, watercress has been particularly singled out for its
health-giving and even cancer-fighting properties. We were not the first to
notice. According to Dr Nicholas Culpeper in *The Compleat Herbal* of 1653:

> Watercress pottage is a good remedy to cleanse the blood in the spring and
> help headaches and consume the gross humours winter has left behind;
> those that would live in health may use it if they please; if they will not,
> I cannot help it. If any fancy not pottage, they may eat the herb as salad.

Eels

Fish arrived in London's Billingsgate market and was eaten by all classes:

> First wash him in water and salt; then pull off his skin below his vent or navel, and not much further. Having done that take out his guts as clean as you can, but wash him not. Then give him three or four scotches with a knife, and then put into his belly and those scotches, sweet herbs, and anchovy and a little nutmeg grated or cut very small … Having done this, pull his skin over him, all but his head, which you are to cut off, to the end you may tie his skin about that part where his head grew … roast him leisurely and baste him with water and salt till his skin breaks, and then with butter; and having roasted him enough, let what was put into his belly and what he drips, be his sauce. When I go to dress an eel thus, I wish he were as long and as big as that which was caught in Peterborough river in the year 1667, which was a yard and three-quarters long. If you will not believe me, then go and see him at one of the coffee houses in King Street in Westminster.

Smoked Eel

From Izaak Walton, *The Compleat Angler*, 1679.

The Character of the Cook

There was even a recipe for the cook herself:

> The cook must be cleanly both in body and garments. She must have a quick eye, a curious nose, a perfect taste, and a ready ear; and she must not be butter-fingered, sweet-toothed, nor faint-hearted. For the first will let everything fall; the second will consume what it should increase; and the last will lose time with too much niceness.

From The English Housewife, 1683.

The Eighteenth Century:

1707: Act of Union passed merging the Scottish and the English Parliaments, thus establishing The Kingdom of Great Britain.

1721: Robert Walpole became the first Prime Minister of Great Britain

Throughout this century farmers began keeping animals though the winter thus meaning that fresh meat was now available all year round

Chapter 6

The
Eighteenth Century

INNOVATIONS in farming continued apace, one of the greatest changes in the Eighteenth Century being that animals were kept through the winter, rather than being slaughtered en masse due to lack of fodder. This, of course, meant that fresh meat, not just salted, was available all year round and cookery was transformed. Transport began to improve too and, as a direct result, food became less regional. Fish, for instance, could be eaten inland. All in all, there was more choice about what you could eat and when you could eat it.

If you had money, it was not just about what you ate, but also about how much. Family dinners were enormous – it wasn't just special occasions that looked as a feast would look to us today. From the Eighteenth Century until the end of the Nineteenth Century, dinner consisted of two courses as a rule, but each course was a dozen or more dishes. Soups, meat, fish, jellies and puddings were all placed on the table at the same time. When there were guests present, there was even more extravagance. It was not just a matter of the food itself, but of how the food was presented and the table decorated. There were pyramids of fruit, sculpted silver and glass to hold candles, sweets or condiments, and other sculptures that were simply to be enjoyed as works of art. Fresh flowers in elaborate arrangements appeared – or sometimes flowers made of silk were used.

The dining room itself would be finely decorated, too. In the *Works* of Robert and James Adam, they scorned the French habit of relying purely on the show of the table and painted a rather different picture of the English dining room and its customs:

> Accustomed by habit or induced by the nature of our climate, we indulge more largely in the enjoyment of the bottle. Every person of rank here is either a member of the legislation, or entitled by his condition to take part in the political arrangements of his country, and to enter with ardour into those discussions to which they give rise; these circumstances lead men to live more with one another, and more detached from the society of the ladies. The eating rooms are considered as the apartments of conversation, in which we are to pass a great part of our time. This renders it desirable to have them fitted up with elegance and splendour, but in a style different from that of other apartments. Instead of being hung with damask, tapestry, they are always finished with stucco, and ordained with statues and paintings, that they may not retain the smell of the victuals.

The victuals were changing, too. Sweet dishes – jellies, custards, blancmanges and so on – now took on such importance that they would be presented as pagodas or desert islands. According to Antonin Carême: 'The fine arts are five in number: to wit, painting, sculpture, poetry, music, architecture – whose main branch is confectionery.'

The architectural quality of these desserts was created by gelatine derived from animals. Because they are sweet it may come as a surprise that jellies and blancmanges use animal products, specifically calves' feet, to provide the jelly to make them set (as they still often do today). They could also be made from ground horn (from deer) or isinglass (made from fish gut). Jaunemanger, as its name suggests, was a more yellow blancmange taking its extra colour from egg yolks. These dishes were hugely popular, especially at balls, where there would be whole tables of sweet dishes, and they would be combined with sherry, brandy, fresh and preserved fruits – even gold leaf.

Elizabeth Raffald gives recipes for such extraordinary sounding Eighteenth Century puddings as 'A Transparent Pudding covered with a Silver Web' and 'A Rocky Island of Gilded Flummery' (flummery is another name for blancmange). While John Farley, cook at the renowned London Tavern, recommends Desert Island:

> Form a lump of paste into a rock three inches broad at the top. Then colour it and set it in the middle of a deep china dish. Set a cast figure on it with a crown on its head, and a knot of rock candy at its feet. Then make a roll of paste an inch thick and stick it on the inner edge of the dish two parts round. Cut eight pieces of eringo roots about three inches long, and fix them upright to the roll of paste on the edge. Make gravel walks of shot comfits round the dish and set small figures in them. Roll out some paste and cut it open like Chinese rails. Bake it and fix it on either side of the gravel walks with gum, and form an entrance where the Chinese rails are, with two eringo roots for pillars.

Not surprisingly, perhaps, such recipes were known as Conceited Dishes.

Except for the grand palaces of the nobility, houses began to shrink in the Eighteenth Century. Elegance rather than grandeur was the order of the day and the great hall was replaced with drawing rooms and dining rooms. The housekeeper, a woman – except in those grand households that boasted a butler – generally ruled this new roost, commanding an army of housemaids and kitchen staff. In elegant households, she also took over many of the roles the lady of the house would previously have undertaken herself. She washed the treasured and delicate porcelain, she took over the still room to make pickles and preserves, where in the past the mistress would have made powders and ointments to heal the sick. The kitchen lost much of its 'physick' role, which

Tea was the most fashionable drink of the century. An expensive choice, it was stored in caddies to keep the tea leaves dry. The word caddy derived from *Kati*, a Malay word for the unit in which tea was measured.

was now handed over to physicians.

This newly idle English gentlewoman of the Eighteenth Century would often be woken by a servant and served a cup of hot chocolate, but the most important drink of the period was, without doubt, tea. First introduced in 1610 it gradually usurped coffee, as the coffee houses gave way to tea gardens. The first were enjoyed only by men, but tea gardens were a meeting place for ladies too.

In 1711, Thomas Twining started to sell tea in packets for domestic use and, in 1740, when import duties on tea were reduced, it became the most fashionable drink of the century. It was still only for the rich, however, being astronomically expensive in spite of the tax reduction. Tea caddies were not just the place to store the leaves to keep them dry and uncontaminated, they were also fitted with locks to keep them away from thieving servants.

Tea began to be served at home after dinner among the ladies while the men stayed in the dining room to drink port. A whole array of new accoutrements was needed for the serving of tea, and while silver was very popular for teapots, the new ceramic factories, such as Wedgwood, were coming into their own. They were soon to create matching sets of teapots, sugar bowls, coffee pots, slop basins, milk jugs and tea drinking bowls, soon replaced by cups with handles and saucers – either as earthenware or the much finer and more expensive porcelain.

Eating Out

In London, one did not always eat at home. There were taverns and chop-houses where you could have turtle soup and scalloped oysters, a chop or a steak. Interestingly, these first restaurants were not for the rich (who went to hotels or were members of clubs) or for the poor who bought food from street hawkers. They were for the emerging middle classes – the clerks who pepper Dickens' novels. It was here, though, that particular dishes were to become embedded in the national psyche for decades, or longer: steak and kidney pudding, toad-in-the-hole, boiled beef and carrots, bubble and squeak, and tripe.

Rules, the famous Covent Garden restaurant, opened as an oyster house in 1798, run by Thomas Rule and his three sons. A rhyme commemorates the early days:

And the three young Rules rush wildly about;
With dozens of oysters and pewters of stout.

There was at the time nothing of the kind in Paris, so when Antoine Beauvilliers opened the first one in 1782, he called it the Grande Taverne de Londres, after the London Tavern where dining out had been celebrated for 100 years.

MEAT, GAME AND POULTRY

Some things were not changing, however. Meat, game and poultry were still all roasted over the fire and we must assume that the fires were very hot indeed. Hannah Glasse and John Farley both recommend that ducks should be roasted for 15 minutes and a goose for just 20 minutes. If the roasting stayed the same, there was experimentation when it came to how the meat was served. Duck could be served with apple or orange sauce, or even an olive sauce in which sliced olives were gently stewed for 20 minutes and then added to a rich gravy. Duck could also be boiled or stewed. Chef John Simpson did this in 1805 at a dinner for the Prince of Wales at Stowe in Buckinghamshire, stewing the ducks in sherry and stock with onions, herbs, bay leaves and mace, and covering them with bacon rashers. He then strained the juices to make a sauce, adding dozens of stoned olives to it.

Chickens could be stuffed with the ubiquitous oysters:

Take pullet chicken, or veal sweetbreads, mushrooms, oysters, anchovies, marrow and a little lemon peel, a little pepper salt nutmeg and a little Thime, marjoram and savory a few each. Mingle all these with the yolk of an egg then raise up the skin of the breast of your fowls and stuff it and then stitch it up again and lard them. Fill their bodies with oysters and roast them. Make good strong gravy sauce. So you may do pheasants, chickens, or what fowls you please.

From *England's Newest Way of Cooking*, Henry Howard, , 1710.

Some cuts of meat that we would never consider having today (always assuming we could find them) were considered the height of elegance in the Eighteenth Century. Jane Austen wrote in a letter to her sister Cassandra on 17 November, 1798, 'I am very fond of experimental housekeeping, such as having an ox-cheek now and

then.' Although it needed long, slow cooking – usually overnight – the result was full of flavour, especially when garnished with globe artichokes, truffles or morels.

Table of Fowl

Most proper and in season for the four quarters of the year Charles Carter's *Complete Cook* (1730) advised what birds and small game to eat when, and this table demonstrates just how far our ancestors would go in search of tasty and often minute quantities of flesh.

March, April, May
Turkeys with eggs
Pheasants with eggs
Partridge with green corn
Pullets with eggs
Green geese
Young ducklings
Tams pidgeons
Squab pidgeons
Young rabbits
Young leverets
Caponetts
Chicken peepers
Young turkeys
Tame ducks
Young rooks
Young sparrows

June, July, August
Ruffs Reeves Godwits
Knots Quails Rayls
Penrets dottrells
Pheasant polts
Young partridges
Heath polts, black or red game
Turkey caponetts
Flacking ducks
Wheat ears
Virgin pullets
Young herons
Young bustards
Pea polts
Wild pigdeons
Young coots

September, October, November	December, January February
Wild ducks	Chickens
Teals	Woodcocks
Willd geese	Snipes
Barganders	Larks
Brandgeese	Plovers
Widgeons	Curlews
Shrilldraks	Redshanks
Cackle ducks	Sea pheasants
Cygnets	Sea parrots
Pheasants	Shuflers
Partridges	Divers
Grouse	Ox eyes
Hares	Peacocks and hens
Ortelans	Bustards
Wild pidgeons	Turkeys
Capons	Geese
Pullets	Blackbirds
	Fedlefares, thrushes

The Invention of Toast

The slices of bread and butter, which they give you with your tea, are as thin as poppy leaves; but there is another kind of bread and butter, usually eaten with tea, which is roasted by the fire and is incomparably good. You take one slice after another and hold it to the fire on a fork till the butter is melted, so that it penetrates a number of slices all at once; this is called 'toast'.

Charles Moritz, a Swiss traveller in England in 1792.

Moritz had clearly never met Hannah Glasse who, in *The Art of Cookery Made Plain and Easy* (1747) took the concept of toast to even greater heights in the form of 'Rabbit' or 'rare-bite':

Toast a slice of bread brown on both sides, then lay it in a plate before the fire. Pour a glass of red wine over it and let it soak the wine up. Then cut some cheese very thin and lay it very thick over the bread and put it in a tin oven before the fire and it will be toasted and browned presently.

SOUPS AND BROTHS

Plain soups and broths had long been known to be very nourishing for invalids, but in the Eighteenth Century – and in extravagant households – they were to become much more elaborate, containing lots of meat and game. Antonin Carême, chef to George IV, had a recipe for hare soup that included Champagne, claret, truffles and quenelles of 30 partridges. Thin, consommé-type soups were known as 'gravies'. Carlton House Soup was one such, flavoured with Madeira wine and served with balls of choux pastry stuffed with game or cheese.

Turtle soup was regarded as a particular luxury. According to Alexis Soyer writing in the following century, it arrived in England in the early Eighteenth Century:

> During the time of the South Sea Bubble, when the female aristocracy partook of the prevalent feature and flocked into the courts and alleys surrounding the Exchange, turtle soup was in the height of fashion, the cost being one guinea per plate.

Bell's Weekly magazine of 1808 records a Spanish Dinner at the London Tavern where 2,500lbs of turtle was consumed by 400 guests. Turtles were transported in fresh water tanks, alive, from the West Indies, and weighed in at 60 to 100lbs. The soup itself was made from the head and lights, while the belly, boiled, and the back, roasted, were served separately. Even the fins made a separate little dish, served in a rich sauce. The thought of turtle soup or any other turtle dish is nauseating to most of us today, as is mock turtle soup – the mock turtle being the head of a calf with the addition of plenty of Madeira wine. Eighteenth Century cooks had no concerns about mad cow disease.

Beau Brummel

Beau Brummel explaining why he had jilted a lady. 'My dear fellow! The thing is impossible, what else could I do? I found she actually ate *cabbage!*'

FRUITS AND VEGETABLES

The walled kitchen garden was still popular in the Eighteenth Century and yielded a great diversity of vegetables, fruits and herbs, some of which are unknown today. English truffles, globe artichoke, damsons and nectarines were all popular. Tomatoes were still a rare luxury and even in the next century, Mrs Beeton regarded them as rather dangerous and likely to cause 'vertigo and vomiting'. The potato, though, had already established itself – there were riots in Ireland when the potato crop failed in 1723.

Artichokes became a particularly popular Regency vegetable, though in the previous century they had gained something of a reputation. According to Nicholas Culpeper in *The Compleat Herbal* of 1653:

> The Latins call them Cinera, only our college calls them Artichocus. They are under the dominion of Venus and therefore it is no marvel if they provoke lust, as indeed they do, being somewhat windy meat: and yet they stay the involuntary course of natural seed in man, which is commonly called nocturnal pollutions.

The modern taste for cooking vegetables, al dente, was also the vogue in the Eighteenth Century. In 1783, John Farley published *The London Art of Cookery*:

> Numbers of Cooks spoil their Garden Stuffs by boiling them too much. All kinds of vegetables should have a little crispness, for if you boil them too much you will deprive them both of their sweetness and beauty.

The English became, too, great picklers of vegetables. In *The Ladies' Assistant* and *Complete System of Cookery* by Mrs Mason in 1773, the following recipes is given for pickled beetroot:

> Boil it till tender, peel it, and if you choose it cut it into shapes. Pour over it a hot pickle of white wine vinegar, a little ginger, pepper and horseradish sliced.

In fact, pickles were just the tip of a very hot iceberg. England was becoming, through its empire, fonder than ever of spicy flavours and catchups (ketchups), pickles, soy sauce and chutneys were eaten with everything. From Regency times commercial bottled sauces were also available. Ketchup (also catsup and catchup) comes from the Malay word kechup – a fish sauce. In England it was mostly based on walnuts or mushrooms. Ginger was brought in a thick syrup by the East Indiamen, stored in stone jars. It became very popular, especially for ice creams and other sweets. Chutney comes from the Hindi word chatni – a pickle. Hannah Glasse, in *The Art of Cookery Made Plain and Easy* (1747) gave a recipe for catchup, which she recommended for the long journeys of ships' captains:

> Take a gallon of strong, stale beer, one pound of anchovies from the pickle, a pound of shallots, peeled, half an ounce of mace, half an ounce of cloves, a quarter of an ounce of whole pepper, three or four larges races of ginger, two quarts of the large mushrooms flaps rubbed to pieces. Cover all this close and let it simmer till it is half wasted then strain it through a flannel bag. Let it stand till it is quite cold, then bottle it. You may carry it to the Indies.

Sorrel

Sorrel has been classified both as a herb and as a vegetable and it was once very popular in England. Now it is little known and in recipes it is generally replaced by spinach, which has a similar taste. It can be cooked, but Eliza Acton recommended using it as a salad, serving it with 'equal portions of very tender lettuce and, when it is not objected to, mixed tarragon may be strewed thickly upon them.' Earlier, T. Hall wrote in *The Queen's Royal Cookery* (1709):

Take a handful or two of sorrel, beat it in a mortar with two pippins pared and quartered. Add thereto a little vinegar and sugar. This is your green sauce to send in saucers. [Pippins are apples.]

TUREENS AND RAISED PIES

Among the great culinary success stories of this period were the tureens and raised pies that became so popular in Regency times and were generally put in pride of place on the supper tables of routs and balls. They comprised all kinds of game, poultry and meat, including whole boned fowl, goose, duckling or even larks, the bird stuffed with tongue or truffles. Without the pastry crust, these dishes were known as 'puptons' or 'mittons'. The pastry was hot water crust, a form of pastry that goes back to the Middle Ages when it was called the coffyn or coffer, meaning the enclosure for the meat within.

The great Eighteenth Century potteries, Wedgwood and Spode, imitated the pie crust by making tureens – casseroles for cooking game with the pot replacing the pie crust itself. The word pâté itself, that now refers to a potted meat (or fish or occasionally vegetable) derives from the word 'pastry'. Originally, the meat would have been baked within a pastry case that was eventually discarded or used again for more baking, but never eaten. The filling took on the name of its container and became known as pate. The English word patty has a similar derivation.

For special occasions, pies could be huge containing whole hams or salmon. They were usually served cold. Any gaps between the meat and the pastry case were filled with forcemeat made from veal, chicken or rabbit and could be highly flavoured with spices, herbs and garlic. These pies remained popular well into the next century:

> I bought the other day a common earthen tureen for which I gave ninepence. I made some forcemeat precisely the same as for pies, boned a grouse and stuffed it as for a pheasant pie, and seasoning the same; I then lined the tureen with the forcemeat, put two pats of butter and a bay leaf upon the top, then placed on the cover, fixing it down with a band of common paste laid inside upon the rim of the tureen, and baked it three hours in a moderate oven, and when I opened it about a week afterwards it was most delicious.

From *The Modern House or Ménagère*, Alexis Soyer, 1850.

SUET

The innovation of the muslin cloth resulted in the rise of the English pudding. While this could be sweet, in the modern sense of pudding, it could also be savoury – whatever the ingredients, the muslin cloth held the spherical pudding together while it steamed. But in both sweet and savoury puddings, suet was the vital ingredient, and a particularly useful one for the hungry bellies of the poor.

In the less wealthy household, where meat was scarce, it was usual to have something filling before you reached the meat course. This was often a suet pudding or a Yorkshire pudding and it would take the edge off the appetite so that less meat would be needed. Mrs Gaskell's Mr Holbrook gave this view of domestic economy in her novel *Cranford*:

> When I was a young man, we used to keep strictly to my father's rule, 'No broth, no ball; no ball, no beef' and always began dinner with broth. Then we had suet puddings, boiled in the broth with the beef: and then we had the meat itself. If we did not sup our broth, we had no ball, which we liked a deal better; and the beef came last of all, and only those had it who had done justice to the broth and the ball. Now folks begin with sweet things and turn their dinners topsy-turvy.

FISH

Shellfish were very popular in the Eighteenth Century and many more fish –and parts of fish – were eaten than are today. A case in point was the delicacy known as the head and shoulders of cod, served with an oyster sauce and decorated with parsley, lemon and horseradish. Mrs Rundell (who was writing her recipes as the Eighteenth Century turned into the Nineteenth Century) in *A New System of Domestic Cookery* considered it:

> a very genteel and handsome dish ... About the head are many delicate

parts, and a great deal of the jelly kind. The jelly lies about the jawbones and the firm parts of the head. Some are fond of the palate, and others of the tongue which likewise may be got by putting a spoon into the mouth.

Mrs Rundell also has recipes for eels, once a very common dish, especially in London where they could be found in plenty in the River Thames – as at the time could salmon. Jellied eels were never made at home but were widely available at jellied eel stalls throughout the capital. They also sold shellfish, particularly whelks, cockles and mussels. They were often served with mashed potato and gravy or could be served inside a hot loaf. Lampreys – fish that are never served nowadays in England – were also popular and were not dissimilar to eels, though smaller. A couple of centuries earlier, Elizabeth I was partial to them and is quoted as saying that 'Lampreys are one of my passions.'

Hannah Glasse suggested treating them like this:

The best of this sort of fish are taken in the River Severn and when they are in season the fishmonger and others in London have them from Gloucester, but if you are where they are to be had fresh you may dress them as you please. To fry lampreys, bleed them and save the blood, then wash them in hot water to take off the skins and cut them in pieces. Fry

In the Eighteenth and Nineteenth Centuries, oysters were the food of the poor and would be eaten hot, bought from street hawkers or restaurants aimed at workers, such as Rules which opened as an oyster house in London's Covent Garden in 1798.

them in a little fresh butter, not quite enough, pour out the fat, put a little white wine, give the pan a shake round season it with whole pepper, nutmeg, salt, sweet herbs and a bay leaf, put in a few capers, a good piece of butter rolled in flour and the blood. Give the pan a shake round often and cover them close. When you think they are enough, take them out. Strain the sauce, then give a boil, quick, squeeze in a little lemon and pour over the fish.

Oysters were not the highly priced rarity they are today. In *The Experienced English Housekeeper*, 1769, Mrs Raffald says:

Take a quarter of a hundred of large oysters, beat the yolks of two eggs, add it to a little nutmeg, and a blade of mace pounded, a spoonful of flour and a little salt, dip in oysters, and fry them in hog's lard a light brown. They are a proper garnish for cod's head, calf's head or most made dishes.

Mackerel were plentiful around the British coastline and Hannah Glasse suggested grilling them, stuffed with mint, parsley and fennel, and serving with a fennel sauce. John Farley in *The London Art of Cookery*, 1783, recommended simmering them in boiling water, and a Cornish Women's Institute recipe from 1773 roasted them with fennel, parsley and gooseberries. Salmon, fresh from the Thames, were grilled on a gridiron by John Farley at the London Tavern, wrapped in writing paper – an Eighteenth Century precursor of the 'en papillote' method.

EIGHTEENTH CENTURY COOKBOOK

Ices

The Regency loved ices – ice creams, custard ices, sorbets – and they were made in special ice cream machines, cooled by freezing salt and ice, and cranked with a handle until they were set. Ice houses were built from the beginning of the century – usually partly or fully underground – where ice could be stored. The ice cream may well have been served with 'A Quire of Paper', which resemble very thin, sweet pancakes:

> To make cream ice. Peel, stone and scald twelve apricots, beat them fine in a mortar, and put to them six ounces of sugar and a pint of scalding cream. Work it through a fine sieve, put it into a tin that hath a close cover and set it in a tub of ice broken small and a large quantity of salt put among it. When you see your cream grow thick around the edges, stir it and set it in again until it is all frozen up. Then put on the lid and have ready another tub with ice and salt as before: put your tin in the middle

and lay ice over and under it: let it stand four or five hours and then dip your tin in warm water before you turn it out. You may use any sort of fruit if you have not apricots, only observe to work it fine.

From *The Experienced English Housekeeper*, Elizabeth Raffald, 1769.

Take 4oz of ginger preserved. Pound it and put it in a basin with two gills of syrup, a lemon squeezed and one pint of cream; then freeze it.

From *The Complete Confectioner*, Frederick Nutt, 1789.

A Quire of Paper

Take to a pint of cream, eight eggs, leaving out two whites, three spoonfuls of fine flour, three spoonfuls of sack [sherry] and one spoonful of orange-flower water, a little sugar, a grated nutmeg, and a quarter of a pound of butter, melted in the cream. Mingle all well together, mixing the flour with a little cream at first, that it may be smooth. Butter your pan for the first pan-cake, and let them run as thin as you can possibly to be whole. When one side is colour'd 'tis enough. Take them carefully out of the pan and strew some fine sifted sugar between each; lay them as even on each other as you can. This quantity will make twenty.

From *A Collection of Receipts*, Mary Kettilby, 1728.

Gilded Fish in Jelly

A typical 'conceited' dish!

Fill two large fish moulds with clear blancmanger. When cold turn them

out and gild them with leaf gold or strew them over with gold and silver bran mixed. Then lay them on a soup dish and fill it with thin clear calf's head jelly, which must be so thin as to admit the fish to swim in it. Lisbon or any kind of pale wine will answer the purpose [of making the jelly].

From *The London Art of Cookery*, John Farley, 1783.

Buttered Shrimps

All kind of shellfish were popular in the Eighteenth Century:

Stew a quart of shrimps with half a pint of white wine, with a nutmeg, then beat four eggs with a little white wine and a quarter of a pound of beaten butter. Then shake them well in a dish [over heat] till they be thick enough. Then serve them with one sippet for a side dish.

From *England's Newest Way of Cookery*, Henry Howard, 1710.

Shrimp was a favoured dish of the Eighteenth Century and could be potted to preserve it for longer.

Wild Sea Samphire on a Cliff Edge

Pickled Sampier

Sampier, or samphire, is a vegetable that grows on salt marshes around Norfolk. While it can be cooked in the same way as asparagus, in the Eighteenth Century it was also pickled:

> Let it be gathered about Michaelmas or in the spring and put two or three hours into a brine of water and salt, then into a clean tinned brass pot with three parts of strong white wine vinegar and one part of water and salt or as much as will cover the sampier, keeping the vapour from issuing out by pushing down the pot lid, and so hang it over the fire for half an hour only. Being taken off let it remain cover'd till it be cold and then put it up into small barrels or jars with the liquor and some fresh vinegar water and salt, and thus it will keep very green. If you be near the sea that water will supply the place of brine. This is the Dover Receit.

> From *Acetaria, a Discourse of Sallets*, John Evelyn, 1706.

Regalia of Cowcumbers

In the Eighteenth Century many vegetables commonly eaten raw today would have been cooked. This recipe takes this approach to cucumbers:

> Take twelve cowcumbers and slice them as for eating: beat and squeeze them very dry. Flour and fry them brown, then put to them claret, gravy, savoury, spice and a bit of butter rouled up in flour. Toss them up thick, they are sauce for mutton or lamb.

> From *Kidder's Receipts*, 1720.

Hampton Court Pupton

This recipe is for the sort of hot tureen that could have been served at a typical Eighteenth Century party:

> Blanch 6 pigeons in boiling water, then lard the breasts and brown the birds in butter or lard. Then stew them in stock just to cover them. When almost tender, add a handful of well-washed mushroom (and of morels if possible), 2 previously blanched sweetbreads cut in pieces and fried, and 12 blanched and peeled whole chestnuts. Let it all simmer until the pigeons are very tender. Meanwhile melt 4oz butter and in it brown 2 whole, peeled onions. Stir in a tablespoonful of flour, brown it and gradually add 2 pints of stock from the pigeons, stirring and heating it till the sauce is smooth and thick. Add the other ingredients and season well with salt, pepper and nutmeg. Let it simmer until most of the liquid has

evaporated leaving a very thick sauce which clings to the meat. Remove from the heat.

Now line a very large buttered terrine with 4 or 5 rashers of bacon as long as your hand and as thin as a shilling, cover the bottom and sides with good forcemeat, half-inch thick and deep enough to make a case for the pigeons and their gravy. Put the birds in breast down and pack the other ingredients round them, add the thick gravy, having removed the onions. Squeeze in the juice of a lemon, and cover the top with forcemeat 1 inch deep, closing it well round the sides. Smooth it well with your hand and brush it over with a beaten egg, then sprinkle the top with bread crumbs. Bake it for an hour in a moderate oven. Before serving loosen the sides with a knife and, holding the serving dish to the top of your fireproof dish, invert them carefully. If well baked it should come away and stand upright like a brown loaf. Squeeze the juice of an orange round it, lay round it fry'd parsley. No sauce is required as there is sauce in the middle.

From *Royal Cookery*, Patrick Lamb, 1710.

Jugged Hare

Cut the hare as for eating, season it with pepper, salt and beaten mace. Put it into a jug or pitcher with a close top. Put to it a bundle of sweet herbs and set it in a kettle of boiling water. Let it stand [on a low heat] till it is tender. Then take it up and pour the gravy into a tossing pan, with a glass of red wine, one anchovy, a large onion stuck with cloves, a little beaten mace and Chyan [cayenne] pepper to your taste. Boil it a little and thicken it. Dish up your hare and strain the gravy over it, then send it up [to the table].

From *The Experienced English Housekeeper*, Elizabeth Raffald, 1769.

Beef à la Mode

Meat was not only roasted. Beef a la mode was very popular in the Eighteenth Century and appears in most cookery books of the period:

Take a fleshy piece of beef. Take out the fat, skins and bone. Then beat it well and flat it with your rowling pin or cleaver. Lard it with fat bacon quite through as long as your meat is deep, and as big as your finger. Then season it high with salt, pepper, beaten nutmeg, cloves and mace. Then put it in a pot where nothing but beef has boiled in good strong beef broth and put in a handful of sweet herbs, a bayleaf, so let it boil till 'tis tender, and if there be no liquor that will make an end of stewing it. Then take up as much as of it you think fit before you put in your wine and other things. Then put all the things in and let it stew till you see the liquor do thicken and taste well of the spice. Then take it up and take out the bayleaves and shallot. You may eat it hot or cold.

From *England's Newest Way of Cookery*, Henry Howard, 1710.

The Nineteenth Century:

1815: Napoleon's defeat at Waterloo brings a conclusion
       to the Napoleonic Wars.

1834: Spanish Inquisition officially ends.

1883: Krakatoa volcano explosion.

1888: Jack the Ripper began murdering.

Chapter 7

The
Nineteenth Century

TEA BECAME England's favourite drink in the Nineteenth Century, affordable to all after decades of being locked away from light fingered servants! The railways meant food could be transported far more quickly within the country and from further afield. In her potted mushrooms recipe, Eliza Acton suggests:

> Persons inhabiting parts of the country where mushrooms are abundant, may send them easily when thus prepared, to their friends in cities, or in less productive counties. If poured into jars, with sufficient butter to cover them, they will travel any distance and can be re-warmed for use.

While the Victorian train network made such gifts possible, cattle were still being driven (that is, walked) to market, even through the streets of central London. On Monday afternoons, Blackfriars Bridge was 'perfectly thronged with cattle and sheep'. The middle classes loved their beef. However, rather like the venison of earlier times, it was rarely seen on the tables of the poor who had a virtually meat-free diet, surviving on little more than bread and cheese, potatoes and porridge.

Food could be stored in cans for the first time and medicine discovered bacteria and the concept of food

Tea continued to have appeal but became more affordable so more households could enjoy. This tea canister featured a Chinaman, depicting the tea's origins.

As its name suggests, the aperitif originated in France – the word first being noted in 1888 in its meaning of a drink before dinner. At first aperitifs were vermouth, but later whisky and gin became popular as did Champagne. Before the invention of the word, though, there were drinks before dinner, most usually sweetened wines.

hygiene. Middle-class cooks could produce meals on the new ovens; meals that were previously only possible in the kitchens of great houses. And gadgets were everywhere – jelly moulds, graters, mincers, potato peelers, pastry cutters.

THE VICTORIANS AT DINNER

Family dinners continued to be enormous: a two course affair with the usual dozen or more dishes making up each one, and all being placed on the table at the same time – but with very particular order. According to a booklet written by Mrs Copley in the 1830s:

> For plain family dinners, soup or pudding is placed at the head of the table and meat at the lower end; vegetables straight on each side of the middle, and sauceboats in the middle, boiled meat at the top, roast meat at the bottom; soup in the middle. Then the vegetables and sauceboats at cross-corners of the middle dish, poultry or veal at top, ham or bacon in the middle; roast beef or mutton at top; roast poultry or game at bottom; vegetables and sauces so disposed that the whole table shall present a covered appearance without being crowded.

Then everything was removed and replaced all over again with the dishes of the second course.

The idea that courses should be served in succession with servants handing out dishes for people to help themselves only became popular towards the latter part of the Nineteenth Century. Popularised by Urbain Dubois, chef to Kaiser Wilhelm I, it was known at first as *service à la russe* and quickly spread as it meant food remained hotter for longer. It also meant you had to be very rich and able to afford the large number of servants needed for this way of dining. By the end of the century, when this method of dining had really taken over, the comparatively empty table was filled with flower decorations – replacing all those dishes.

A little lower down the social scale, food was still a source of delight and anticipation. In *The Old Curiosity Shop*, Charles Dickens conjured up the joys of tripe:

> A mighty fire was blazing on the hearth and roaring up the chimney with a cheerful sound, which a large cauldron, bubbling and simmering in the heat, lent its pleasant aid to swell ... Mr Codlin sat smiling in the

The Banqueting Room of Brighton Pavilion from Nash's Views, designed by Robert Jones.

chimney corner, eyeing the landlord as with a roguish look he held the cover in his hand, and, feeling that his doing so was needful to the welfare of the cookery, suffered the delightful stream to tickle the nostrils of his guest. The glow of the fire was upon the landlord's bald head, and upon his twinkling eye, and upon his watering mouth, and upon his pimpled face, and upon his round fat figure. Mr Codlin drew his sleeve across his lips, and said in a murmuring voice, 'What is it?'

'It's a stew of tripe,' said the landlord, smacking his lips, 'and cow-heel' smacking them again, 'and bacon' smacking them once more 'and steak' smacking them for the fourth time 'and peas, cauliflowers, new potatoes, and sparrow grass, all working up together in one delicious gravy.' Having come to the climax, he smacked his lips a great many times, and taking a long hearty sniff of the fragrance that was hovering about, put on the cover again with the air of one whose toils on earth were over.

'At what time will it be ready?' asked Mr Codlin faintly.

'It'll be done to a turn,' said the landlord looking up to the clock – the very clock had a colour to its fat white face, and looked a clock for Jolly

The Banqueting Room at Brighton Pavilion, the epitome of the Regency era, as
visitors can see it today.

Sandboys to consult – 'it'll be done to a turn at twenty-two minutes before eleven.'

'Then,' said Mr Codlin, 'fetch me a pint of warm ale, and don't let nobody bring into the room even so much as a biscuit till the time arrives.'

In spite of the seeming extravagance, Victorian England also had a 'waste not, want not' attitude to cooking. Eliza Acton in her 1845 *Modern Cookery for Private Families*, explained it thus:

> It may safely be averred that good cookery is the best and truest economy, turning to full account every wholesome article of food, and converting into palatable meals, what the ignorant either render uneatable, or throw away in disdain.

Certainly, the Victorians like their predecessors, ate much more of any beast than we generally do today. William Cobbett wrote *Cottage Economy* in 1824 to advise the poor how to make full use of a pig – an animal not usually considered genteel enough for the gentry, but good enough for farmers and rough country folk:

> If the wife be not a slattern … in the mere offal, in the mere garbage, there is food, and delicate food, too, for a large family for a week, and hogs' puddings for the children, and some for the neighbours' children who come to play with them. For these things are by no means to be overlooked, seeing that they tend to the keeping alive of that affection in children for their parents, which in later life, will be found absolutely necessary to give effect to wholesome precept, especially when opposed to the boisterous passions of youth. The butcher, the next day, cuts the hog up; and then the house is filled with meat! Souse, griskins, bladebones, thigh-bones, spare-ribs, chines, belly pieces, cheeks all coming into use one after the other, and the last of the latter not before the end of about four or five weeks.

Miss Acton advises on 'the art of preparing good, wholesome, palatable soups, *without great expense* [her italics] though Victorian soups tended to be much more substantial than those we know today and often very meaty or even fishy. In the winter, they would be thickened with 'semoulina, pearl barley, or other ingredients of the same nature' and thus help the cook 'in furnishing comfortable meals in a very frugal manner'.

Soups and broths were also the recommended diet for invalids and Eliza particularly recommends Baron Liebeg's Receipt:

> This admirable preparation is not only most valuable as a restorative of the best kind for invalids who require light but highly nutritious diet, it is also of the utmost utility for the general purposes of the kitchen … The economist who may consider it expensive, must remember that drugs and medical advice are usually far more so.

The recipe itself does not much resemble a present day soup.

> Take a pound of good, juicy beef (rumpsteak is best for the purpose), from which all the skin and fat that can possibly be separated from it, has been cut away. Chop it up small like sausagemeat; then mix it thoroughly with an exact pint of cold water, and place it on the side of the stove to heat *very slowly indeed*; and give it an occasional stir. It may stand two or three hours before it is allowed to simmer, and will then require at the utmost but fifteen minutes of gentle boiling. Professor Liebeg directs even less time than this, but the soup then occasionally retains a raw flavour which is distasteful. Salt should be added when the boiling first commences, and for invalids, this, in general, is the only seasoning required. When the extract is thus far prepared, it may be poured into a basin, and allowed to stand until any particles of fat it may exhibit on the surface can be skimmed off entirely, and the sediment has subsided and left the soup quite clear (which it speedily becomes), when it may be poured gently off, heated in a clean saucepan, and served at once. It will contain all the nutriment which the meat will yield.

Soups were not just for the poor or the sick. 'Mademoiselle Jenny Lind's Soup' contained pearl sago, cream and egg yolks added to the beef stock and was found by the famous singer to be 'soothing to the chest and beneficial to the voice'. Lord Mayor's Soup had pigs' ears and feet 'from which the hair has been carefully removed' together with half a pint of sherry or Madeira. Even carrot soup used beef stock.

The exception to the gentry not eating pork was the Christmas boar's head, favourite centre-piece of the Victorian festive table and also in various Oxford colleges, where it is piped in to this day. The head was pickled for a week after certain parts have been removed, such as the eyes and the brain. After pickling,

The Great Kitchen at Brighton Pavilion as it looks today, retaining the style of the Regency era.

the head was stuffed with a rich forcemeat containing the brains, herbs and other flavourings. It was then sewn up and boiled for around six hours, glazed and 'dressed' with prunes for the eyes and a lemon in the mouth. Placed on a large dish, it was sometimes given an Elizabethan ruff to complete the picture.

If the pig was generally regarded as too lowly a beast to be served on the dinner tables of the wealthy, it nevertheless had its uses. Although truffles are nowadays associated almost exclusively with France and Italy (and with astronomical prices), they were also available in England in the Nineteenth Century and the first half of the Twentieth Century. Mostly found in Hampshire, Wiltshire and Kent, they were not so large as the continental truffles, but the method for finding them was the same – a hog would sniff them out and its owner would dig them up.

High Tea was an entirely new meal and it became immensely popular. Mrs Beeton commented:

> In some houses it is a permanent institution quite taking the place of late supper, and to many it is a most enjoyable meal, young people preferring it to dinner, it being a movable feast that can be partaken of at hours which will not interfere with tennis, boating and other amusements, and but little formality is needed. At the usual High Tea there are probably to be found one or two small hot dishes, cold chickens or game, tongue, or ham, salad, cakes of various kinds, some cold fruit tarts with cream or custard and fresh fruits.

This could be served with tea and coffee or with wine.

Even breakfast in the Victorian house was enormous. At around eight o'clock, salmon with mashed potatoes, grilled pheasant, sheeps' trotters, tripe and onions, curried eggs, cold and cured meats, game pies, steak, black pudding and mutton chops were among the many dishes to be laid out on the sideboard.

PREPARATION IS ALL

Eliza Acton began *Modern Cookery for Private Families* not, as today's cookbooks do, with meals as they are served – with the first course coming first and so on – but with food as it is prepared. Eliza's chapter one, then, is on trussing – a perfect illustration of how very much more hands on Nineteenth Century cooks were. 'Before a bird is trussed,' she says, 'the skin must be entirely freed from any down which may be on it, and from all the stubble-ends of the feathers; the hair also must be singed from it with lighted writing paper, care being taken not to smoke nor blacken it in the operation.'

She goes on to explain what to do with the poultry heads and feet, livers and gizzards and what needles to use to sew them up, once stuffed. Detailed instructions on carving follow because 'the uncouth operations of bad carvers occasion almost as much discomfort to those who witness, as they do generally of awkwardness and embarrassment to those who exhibit them.' Explanations – with drawings showing where to slice – include turbot: 'the rich gelatinous skin … and a portion of the thick part of the fins should be served with every slice'; sucking pig: 'every part of a sucking pig is good, but some persons consider the flesh of the neck which lies between the shoulders and the ribs as the most delicate portion'; loin of veal: 'a slice of the kidney and of the fat which surrounds it should accompany the veal'; she recommends boning a calf's head or it will 'recall too forcibly the appearance of the living animal [which is] very uninviting'; a pheasant 'was formerly always sent to table with the head on, but it was a barbarous custom which has been partially abandoned of late in the best houses'.

To Boil a Calf's Head

When the head is dressed with the skin on, which many persons prefer, the ear must be cut off quite close to it; it will require three quarters of an hour or upwards of additional boiling, and should be served covered with fried crumbs: the more usual mode, however, is to boil it without the skin. In either case first remove the brain, wash the head delicately clean, and soak it for a quarter of an hour; cover it plentifully with cold water, remove the scum as it rises with great care, throw in a little salt, and boil the head gently until it is perfectly tender. In the mean time, wash and soak the brains first in cold and then in warm water, remove the skin or film, boil them in a small saucepan from fourteen to sixteen minutes, according to their size, and when they are done, chop and mix them with eight or ten sage leaves boiled tender and finely minced; or, if preferred, with boiled parsley instead; warm them in a spoonful or two of melted butter, or white sauce; skin the tongue, trim off the root, and serve it in a small dish with the brains round it. Send the head to table very hot with parsley and butter poured over it, and some more in a tureen. A cheek of bacon, or very delicate pickled pork, is the usual accompaniment to boiled calf's head.

From *Modern Cookery for Private Families*, Eliza Acton.

'Creatures of the inferior races eat and drink; only man dines'

Mrs Beeton.

MRS BEETON

While there were many fine cookery books and writers in the Nineteenth Century, the first name that always springs to mind when the subject of Victorian cookery is raised is that of Mrs Isabella Beeton. Though she knew nothing about cookery when she married, she learned quickly – using sources that ranged from Eliza Acton and Mrs Rundell (often unacknowledged) to Dr Kitchener's *Cook's Oracle* and recipes gleaned from the housekeepers of great houses. She was just 23 when her first book, *The Book of Household Management*, was published in serial form and it was her husband Samuel

Beeton, a publisher of books, magazines and paper patterns for dressmaking, who is thought to have had the idea for the great work. She died of puerperal fever, aged just 29.

Mrs Beeton not only produced recipes for every occasion, she explained how to furnish a flat, manage your servants, choose cuts of meat and carve them at the table, and she was, like many cooks and housekeepers, deeply concerned with hygiene and cleanliness. However, it wasn't just washing the equipment that she recommended:

> Do not scrub the inside of your frying pans, unless they be of enamelled iron, as, after this operation, any preparation fried is liable to catch or burn in the pan. If the pan has become black inside, rub it with a hard crust of bread, and wash in hot water, mixed with a little soda.
>
> Have vegetables gathered from the garden at an early hour, so that there is ample time to search for caterpillars, etc. These disagreeable additions need never make their appearance on table in cauliflowers or cabbages, if the vegetable in its raw state is allowed to soak in salt and water for an hour or so.

It is remarkable, in fact, how much of Mrs Beeton's writing is about subjects other than cookery. She gives a very clear view of the work done by the housewife or mistress and her servants. From beauty tips to cleaning bicycles, from dry cleaning ostrich feathers to making use of tea leaves, she has advice on all. Sir Arthur Conan Doyle in his study of married life, *A Duet, with an Occasional Chorus*, has his angel say, 'Mrs Beeton must have been the finest housekeeper in the world. Therefore, Mr Beeton must have been the happiest and most comfortable man.' The angel in the home, indeed. Some of Mrs Beeton's household 'recipes':

Arms, to Whiten

> Rub a slice of ripe tomato over the arms 2 or 3 times a day, and then massage the juice well into the skin with the palms of the hands. Let it dry on, and then wash off with clear water, in which a little borax has been dissolved. Follow this with an application of pure cold cream or a mixture of glycerine and rosewater.

Bicycles, to Clean and Store

> After a ride, and while the mud and dust are quite fresh, brush the

machine thoroughly. Clean the chain with paraffin, and oil very slightly with cycle oil, taking care to wipe carefully afterwards, or dust will accumulate on the oil and clog the machine. Wash the enamelled and plated parts, dry carefully and polish the latter with plate powder. Avoid wetting the tyres. In storing a bicycle away for the winter, cover the metal parts with Vaseline. If the room in which the bicycle is to be kept is very dry, keep a basin of water there. A moist atmosphere will generally prevent the tyres from spoiling.

Ostrich Feathers

To dry-clean and curl an ostrich feather hold it in sulphur fumes. This should be done in the open air, for if any silver or gilt articles are within reach of the fumes they will become tarnished. To dress an ostrich feather without curling is not a difficult task, provided the plume is a good one, and the fronds long and unbroken. A good soap lather should be made, the feather dipped in it, and then squeezed gently between the fingers so as to eliminate the dirt. When it is quite clean it should be rinsed in cold water and then laid flat on a clean towel. The feather should then be dabbed rapidly with a soft handkerchief until the fronds are once more light and fluffy.

Tea Leaves, use of

Tea leaves can be put to various uses in a household. They can be sprinkled over carpets and so help to collect and fix dust. Tea leaves kept for several days, infused with boiling water and then strained make a useful polish for mirror, windows, glasses, varnished wood and furniture and cost nothing. Tea leaves boiled up in fish pans will also remove the smell of the fish.

FISH – AND CHIPS

The national dish of fish and chips – the fish fried in batter – did not appear till the end of the Nineteenth Century. One theory is that it was based on the Italian *fritto misto mare* and was imported by Italian immigrants, at first being sold from hand carts. Boiled peas (or mushy peas) were a popular accompaniment. Peas were sold on the streets of London (and in many other parts of the country) in the Nineteenth Century. They were cooked, like mangetouts today, inside the pods, then dipped in melted butter and eaten by sliding the peas out of the pod with the teeth. Pease pudding was a very popular way to cook peas in Victorian times, and Mrs Beeton had a recipe that recommended soaking then cooking the peas in rainwater for two-and-a-half hours:

> When the peas are tender, take them up and drain. Rub them through a colander with a wooden spoon. Add the butter, eggs, pepper and salt. Beat all well together for a few minutes until the ingredients are well incorporated. Then tie them tightly in a floured cloth. Boil the pudding for another hour, turn it on to the dish and serve very hot. The pudding should always be sent to table with boiled pork.

Fish was also common at breakfast in Victorian times. Finnan haddock was popular but the most typical dish was kedgeree. This fish curry was, of course, an adaptation of an Indian dish and one of many influences to come from

Britain's empire:

> Boil 4oz of rice and put it in a sieve to drain. When quite dry put it in a stewpan with a pound of either cold salmon, cod, whiting or haddock pulled into flakes … Add 3 hard-boiled eggs, cut into quarters, 3oz butter, a dessertspoonful of pepper and salt. Simmer over a clear fire until quite hot. Sprinkle a dessertspoonful of dry curry powder over it. Serve it in a very hot entrée dish.

> From *The Pytchley Book of Refined Cookery*, Major L., 1885.

Eels were still very popular. Eliza Acton observed:

> Eels should be alive and brisk in movement when they are purchased, but the 'horrid barbarity' as it is truly designated, of skinning and dividing them while they are so, is without excuse, as they are easily destroyed by piercing the spinal marrow close to the back part of the skull with a sharp pointed knife or skewer. If this be done in the right place all motion will instantly cease.

But she also had recipes for fish that would probably be more palatable to us today, such as Salmon a la St Marcel (in a spicy cream sauce), baked mackerel, roast red mullet, and red herrings (sprinkled with cayenne).

Of course, it was still oysters that ruled supreme. They were still not regarded as a luxury food. In Dickens' time, they were in plentiful supply and enjoyed by those on lower incomes. His clerk, Mr Guppy, in *Bleak House*, had them for lunch in his local hostelry on a regular basis. Unlike today, when they are generally eaten raw with a squeeze of lemon, they were cooked, often in such hearty dishes as Lancashire Hotpot, where they were combined with mutton, potato and onion, or Steak, Kidney and Oyster Pudding. Traditionally, oysters are eaten only when there is an 'r' in the month (from September to April), but perhaps this was a health consideration – seafood usually being avoided in the hottest months when it was most likely to spoil.

Miss Acton further observed:

> The old-fashioned plan of *feeding* oysters, with a sprinkling of oat-meal or flour, in addition to the salt and water to which they were committed, has long been rejected by all genuine amateurs of these nutritious and excellent fish, who consider the plumpness which the oysters are supposed

to gain from the process, but poor compensation for the flavour which they are sure to lose.

The Victorians preferred their oysters cooked and hot – scalloped oysters, stewed oysters, curried oysters and even oyster sausages were popular.

CONTROLLING THE FIRE

Poultry, meat and game were still usually roasted over an open fire in Victorian times, although ranges began to be introduced in the latter part of the century. Cooking over an open fire was popular in part because the wood often gave a distinctive and desirable flavour, and by no means everyone had access to a range cooker. Spits which could be turned over the fire so that the meat would roast evenly were enhanced with every mechanism Victorian ingenuity could produce, including clockwork, weights and chains.

For roasting meat, Eliza Acton mentions the smoke jack, prevalent in large kitchens that had several turning-spits; the spring jack, the advantage of which was that it cooked with a smaller fire, 'the heat being strongly reflected from the screen upon the meat: in consequence of this, it should never be placed very close to the grate, as the surface of the joint would then become dry and hard.' Then there is the bottle jack, which suspended the meat vertically. She recommends it starts off far from the fire and is only moved nearer when it is two-thirds cooked. All of these roasting methods required a great deal of work, basting the joint with the juices – or dripping – constantly, turning the spit and checking that the meat is evenly cooked and doesn't burn. 'Roasting,' says Eliza, 'requires unremitting attention on the part of the cook rather than any great exertion of skill.'

Steak would be cooked, according to Major L. in the *Pytchley Book of Refined Cookery*, extremely rare. Taken 'from a well-hung rump of beef one inch and a half thick, this in good oxen should be about four pounds', it would then be cooked for just five minutes on one side, followed by just browning the other. It was served with those oysters again, as a sauce. Of course, the Major may have been using a new piece of culinary equipment known as a Conjuror. The steak would be placed inside the machine and a lighted paper put in the section below it. According to Eliza Acton, steak or cutlets would cook in around eight to ten minutes with just two sheets of paper and would then be 'remarkably tender and very palatable.'

Steaming became popular in Victorian times and there were many new labour saving inventions to help 'so admirably constructed and so complete, that the process may be conducted on an extensive scale with very slight trouble to the cook; and with the further advantage of being at a distance from the fire, the steam being conveyed by pipes to the vessels intended to receive it', according to Eliza Acton. Early toasters (for both meat and bread) were devised with racks or hooks on stands to be placed before the fire.

The practicalities of cooking in the early Victorian kitchen involved complexities that we cannot even imagine today. The fire – even when it was a range – governed all culinary matters, and getting it right was an art in itself. Before the cook could even begin to think about inventive dishes and delicate sauces, she had to wrestle with the problem of controlling the blaze. Eliza goes on:

> The common cooking stoves in this country, as they have hitherto been constructed, have rendered the exact regulation of heat which stewing requires rather difficult; and the smoke and blaze of a large coal fire are very unfavourable to many other modes of cookery as well.

NINETEENTH CENTURY COOKBOOK

To Pot Anchovies

Scrape the anchovies very clean, raise the flesh from the bones and pound it to a perfect paste in a Wedgwood or marble mortar, then with the back of a wooden spoon press it through a hair sieve reversed. Next, weight the anchovies and pound them again with double their weight of the freshest butter that can be procured, a high seasoning of mace and Cayenne, and a small quantity of finely grated nutmeg. Set the mixture by in a cool place for three or four hours to harden it before it is put into the potting pans. If butter be poured over, it must only be lukewarm, but the anchovies will keep well for two or three weeks without.

of finely-chopped suet, 1 tablespoon of finely-chopped ham or parboiled chickens' livers, 1 tablespoonful of chopped mushrooms (preferably fresh ones), 1 dessertspoonful of finely-chopped parsley, ¼ of a teaspoonful of finely-grated lemon-rind, ¼ of a teaspoonful of powdered mixed herbs, 1 egg, a good pinch of nutmeg, ½ a teasoonful of salt, ¼ of a teaspoonful of pepper.

Method – Bone the larks and stuff them with the farce, brush them over with the beaten egg and coat them carefully with bread crumbs seasoned with a little salt and pepper. Grill over a clear fire for about 10 minutes and as soon as the bread crumbs are set, brush them lightly over with oiled butter. Serve on croutes.

Mutton Cutlets Braised

The Victorians would have been surprised by our preference for lamb. They ate mostly mutton, which they felt had a superior flavour:

Ingredients – 8 or 10 cutlets from the best end of the neck, larding bacon, 1½oz of butter, ½ a pint of stock, 1 onion, 1 carrot, 1 or 2 strips of celery, ½ a small turnip, a bouquet-garni (parsley, thyme, bay-leaf), glaze, salt and pepper, ⅓ of a pint of tomato or demi-glace sauce, peas, spinach or other vegetable garnish.

Method – Trim and flatten the cutlets into a good shape and insert 5 or 6 fine lardoons, or pieces of fat bacon used for larding, in the lean part of each one. Slice the vegetables, put them into a stewpan with the butter and bouquet-garni, lay the cutlets on the top, put on the lid, and cook gently for about 20 minutes. Have the stock boiling, pour into the stewpan as much of it as will three-quarters cover the vegetables, and add the remainder of the stock as that in the pan reduces. Cover the cutlets with a greased paper, put on the lid, and cook gently for about 50 minutes on the stove or in the oven. When done, brush over one side with meat-glaze, and put them into a hot oven for a few minutes to crisp the bacon. Arrange them in a close circle on a border of potato, serve with the prepared vegetables in the centre and pour round the sauce.

From *Family Cookery*, Mrs Beeton.

Hare, Hashed

The Victorians generally – and Mrs Beeton in particular – were great believers in domestic economy. Nothing was thrown away, it was always re-used:

Ingredients – Remains of cold roast hare, 3/4 of a pint of brown sauce, 1 glass of port or claret (optional), salt and pepper, redcurrant jelly.

Method – Cut the hare into neat slices and put these aside while the bones and trimmings are being boiled for stock. Make the brown sauce, and, when economy is an object, use stock, or equal parts of stock and stout instead of adding wine to the sauce when finished. Season the sauce to taste, put in the slices of hare, let them remain until thoroughly hot, then serve with redcurrant jelly.

From *Family Cookery*, Mrs Beeton.

Okra

One of the many vegetables grown in parts of the Victorians' far-flung empire, okra was brought back to be enjoyed at home:

This plant is a native of the West Indies, although now largely cultivated in India and America. The young, green pods are sometimes pickled, and the older pods are preserved in tins for export. Those imported resemble gherkins in size, but their ends form a sharper point: their colour is lighter and less vivid in tone and their pods contain seeds not unlike pearl barley. Okra has a peculiar flavour, often disagreeable to an unaccustomed palate, and it is exceedingly mucilaginous, the pods in the tin being surrounded by a substance of greater viscidity than gum.

Ingredients – 24 fresh okras, 2 tablespoonfuls of oiled butter, 2 tablespoonfuls of cream or milk, salt and pepper.

Method – Wash the okras in cold water, drain them well, and trim both ends. Place them in a saucepan containing boiling salted water, boil gently for about 15 minutes or until tender and drain well. Make the butter and cream or milk hot in a stewpan, put in the okras, sprinkle liberally with pepper, add a little salt, shake them over the fire for a few minutes, then serve.

From *Family Cookery*, Mrs Beeton.

Flowers

Salad with nasturtiums:

Put a plate of flowers of the nasturtium in a salad bowl, with a tablespoonful of chopped chervil; sprinkle over with your fingers half a teaspoonful of salt, two or three tablespoonfuls of olive oil, and the juice of a lemon; turn the salad in the bowl with a spoon and fork until well mixed, and serve.

From *The Turkish Cookery Book*, Turabi Efendi, 1864.

Cowslip Wine

Ingredients – 4 quarts of cowslip flowers, 4 quarts of water, 3lb of loaf sugar, the finely-grated rind and juice of 1 orange and 1 lemon, 2 tablespoonfuls of brewers' yeast, or $1/4$ of an oz. of compressed yeast moistened with water, $1/4$ of a pint of brandy, if liked.

Method – Boil the sugar and water together for about $1/2$ an hour, skimming when necessary, and pour, quite boiling, over the rinds and strained juice of the

A mahogany box containing a set of six gilt enriched decanters. Similar to a Tantalus, this would be kept locked with only the trusted butler having the key to ensure it was kept full for the master and guests to enjoy. Drinks would include port and brandy.

Hunting, that popular Victorian past-time, might start and end with a sociable drink in a pub.

orange and lemon. Let it cool, then stir in the yeast and cowslip flowers, cover with a cloth, and allow it to remain undisturbed for 48 hours. Turn the whole into a clean dry cask, add the brandy, bung closely, let it remain thus for 8 weeks, then draw it off into clean, dry bottled. Cork the bottles securely, store in a cool, dry place for 3 or 4 weeks, and the wine will then be ready for use.

From *Family Cookery*, Mrs Beeton.

Mango Chutney

The Victorians' favourite chutney, adapted from the Indian recipes:

Ingredients – 50 green mangoes, 6 pints of vinegar, 3lb of sugar, 2lb of tamarinds stoned, 1lb of raisins stoned, 1lb of green ginger sliced, 1 good teaspoonful of powdered cinnamon, 1 level teaspoonful of nutmeg, 1lb of salt.

Method – Peel and slice the mangoes thinly, sprinkle over them the salt, let them remain 36 hours, then drain well. Make a syrup by boiling together 3 pints of vinegar and the sugar. Put the remainder of the vinegar into a preserving-pan, add the mangoes, boil up, simmer gently for about 10 minutes, then add the tamarinds, raisins, ginger, cinnamon and nutmeg. Cook very slowly for about $\frac{1}{2}$ an hour, adding the syrup gradually during the last 10 minutes. Stir and boil the mixture until the greater part of the syrup is absorbed, then turn into bottles, cork securely, and store in a cool, dry place.

Cardamom and other Indian spices reflected Britain's trade with its Empire.

The Twentieth Century:
14 April, 1912: RMS Titanic sink on her maiden voyage.

28 June, 1914: Franz Ferdinand's assassination in Sarajevo marks the begining of the First World War.

1 September, 1939: Germany invades Poland marking the begining of the Second World War.

20 July, 1969: Neil Armstrong becomes the first man to walk on the moon

Chapter 8

The
Twentieth Century

THE TWENTIETH Century saw more changes in the story of food and the way that it is eaten than the entire previous millennium. At the turn of the century, malnutrition was commonplace in the UK. The shocking condition of many army recruits during the First World War meant that, in 1917–18, 41 per cent of them were graded unfit to undergo physical exertion and only 36 per cent were passed as fit for full military service. Less than 100 years later, the Western world faced an obesity epidemic.

Having finally severed the link between medicine and the kitchen, the existence of vitamins was discovered for the first time, though many more years would pass before their importance in everyday diets was realised. Food became increasingly commercialised. In the second half of the century, huge companies – supermarkets and fast-food outlets – provided the diet of vast numbers of people who grew further and further away from cooking and from any concept of the origin of raw ingredients. At the same time, food became global. You could have a MacDonald's in Kathmandu, sushi in Los Angeles, popadoms in London and pasta in South America.

At the beginning of the Twentieth Century, the divide between rich and poor and the diets that they ate was as great as ever. However, whereas in the past, most poor people at least had a place to grow vegetables or keep a few chickens, now the majority of them in the industrialised world were based in cities. Wealthy Edwardians, however, were still living in the style of their Victorian forebears. Harold Nicolson wrote in *Small Talk* of a typical country house breakfast around 1910:

> Only the really improper Edwardians had breakfast in their rooms. The others met, on that Sunday morning, in the dining-room. The smell of last night's port had given place to the smell of this morning's spirits of wine. Rows of little spirit lamps warmed rows of large silver dishes. On a table to the right between the windows were grouped Hams, Tongues, Galantines, Cold Grouse, ditto Pheasant, ditto Partridge, ditto Ptarmigan. No Edwardian meal was complete without Ptarmigan. Hot or Cold. Just Ptarmigan. There would also be a little delicate rectangle of pressed beef from the shop of M. Benoit. On a further table, to the left between the doors, stood fruits of different calibre, and jugs of cold water, and jugs of lemonade. A fourth table contained porridge utensils. A fifth coffee, and pots of Indian and China tea. The latter were differentiated from each other by little ribbons of yellow (indicating China) and of red (indicating, without *arriere pensee*, our Indian Empire). The centre table, which was prepared for twenty-three people, would be bright with Malmaisons and toast-racks. No newspapers were, at that stage, allowed …
>
> Edwardian breakfasts were in no sense a hurried proceeding. The porridge was disposed of negligently, people walking about and watching the rain descend upon the Italian garden. Then would come whiting and omelette and devilled kidneys and little fishy messes in shells. And then tongue and ham and a slice of Ptarmigan. And then scones and honey and marmalade. And then a little melon, and a nectarine or two, and just one or two of those delicious raspberries. The men at that stage would drift (I employ the accepted term) to the smoking-room. The women would idle in the saloon watching the rain descend upon the Italian garden. It was then 10.30.

Behind these gilded scenes, Europe had already started on its inexorable road to war. In 1914, as war broke out, there was a wave of panic buying and hoarding

1920-30s Watercress Harvests

Men and women worked alongside each other at the watercress farms, using traditional methods which have not changed over the centuries.

Vitamins

While wholesome and medicinal foods had been in use for centuries as a way of preserving health and curing illness, in the Twentieth Century, the link between the kitchen and health was mostly severed. The break was almost complete after the discovery of penicillin and its extensive use during the Second World War, when it is thought to have saved around 12–15 per cent of lives that would otherwise have been lost due to infected wounds. The magic bullet of antibiotics had arrived.

However, there were problems that even penicillin couldn't overcome. Scurvy, a particularly unpleasant disease that leads to bleeding gums, severe pain and even death, had for centuries beset sailors who went on long voyages without access to fresh fruit and vegetables. In the Eighteenth Century it was discovered that if the sailors took lemons and limes with them, the incidence of scurvy fell dramatically due to their high vitamin C content – though at that point the existence of vitamins had not been discovered. Captain Cook was an early advocate but the practice was not widely adopted. It did, however, lead to the nickname 'Limeys' for British sailors.

At the very end of the Nineteenth Century, Christiaan Eijkman discovered that eating unpolished rice, rather than the husked polished variety, prevented the disease beriberi. It seemed as if there was some unidentified element in certain foods – beyond the proteins, fats and carbohydrates that were already known – that could have a direct and positive effect on health. Gradually, the concept of vitamins emerged.

It was during research for diseases of deprivation and deficiencies that a clearer picture of vitamins gradually came into focus. In the twenties, thirties and forties, first vitamin C was isolated and shown to be ascorbic acid and then vitamins A, D and K. By the start of the Second World War, awareness of the importance of vitamins had grown to such an extent that, to overcome the privations of rationing, young children's diets were boosted with orange juice, blackcurrant and rosehip syrups, as well as cod liver oil.

as food prices began to rise steadily. In Germany 'war bread' was made by adding rye and potato flour to the mix and there were restrictions on the hours that bread could be either baked or sold. By January 1915, bread was rationed in Germany – everyone had a daily allowance of 8oz (225g). Potatoes and meat were scarce too and prices soared. In Britain, even though there was no real scarcity, food prices still rose steeply. Between August 1914 and July 1915, the average increase in food prices was 34 per cent while particular foods such as sugar, which had risen by 68 per cent, were taken under government control. France also, saw price rises without any real scarcity.

The ladies who had been eating the ptarmigan just a few short years earlier, were now employed in patriotic work such as munitions, which became, according to Mrs Pankhurst, 'the latest society craze'. The *Manchester Guardian* had a story about one such titled lady who celebrated completing her first month of work by inviting a duchess, the wife of a Cabinet Minister, and a working-class colleague called Mabel, to dinner. The table was covered with oil-cloth and the plainest of meals was served. The butler had been sent to the theatre to get him out of the way. It is hard to imagine a sharper contrast and, indeed, it was the first war that ushered in women doing 'men's work' (albeit at a fraction of the wages), new and more unencumbered clothes to do it in, and a separation from the kitchen and the house that could never be reforged. And though many women stopped working after the war – preferential treatment being given to male applicants for jobs – things would never be the same again. Women acquired greater earning power and, with it, greater independence. Most importantly for those living and dining in grand country houses, those employed in residential domestic service left in droves, never to return. From now on it was hard even for the wealthiest to get the staff.

By 1917, food supplies in Britain were in danger. German submarines had sunk hundreds of thousands of tons of food making its way to England across the Atlantic, there was a poor potato harvest and shortages of sugar and wheat. Posters appeared in London with such rallying cries as 'Eat Less Bread and Victory is Secure'. The Board of Agriculture put three million more acres under cultivation, worked by women Land Army volunteers. Allotments flourished and gardens were turned over to vegetables. Nevertheless, outside the shops of butchers, bakers, greengrocers and grocers, the queues grew longer, while inside the prices rose and the choice diminished. Even in middle-class homes, tables looked bare compared to their pre-war splendour. A typical day might see porridge made without milk for breakfast, tea with milk and sugar, and some potatoes fried in fat. Midday dinner might comprise salt brisket of beef, carrots and potatoes, followed by a milk pudding and cheese. Tea would be bread and jam, supper semolina. Voluntary rationing was introduced in the autumn of 1917 and it was formalised into a national scheme the following year.

Wastage, or what was regarded as improper use of food, was punishable by fines or even imprisonment:

> It became a crime for a workman to leave a loaf behind on the kitchen shelf of the cottage from which he was moving (£2 fine), for a maiden lady in Dover to keep fourteen dogs and give them bread and milk to eat (£5), for another lady in Wales to give meat to a St. Bernard (£20), for a furnaceman dissatisfied with his dinner to throw chip potatoes on the fire (£10), and for a lady displeased with her husband to burn stale bread upon her lawn (£5)… A Lincolnshire farmer finding himself able to buy seven stone of rock cakes cheaply from an Army canteen used them to feed pigs; as the food executive officer and a police sergeant were able to pick some of the cakes out of a swill-tub and taste them without bad consequences, the farmer was fined £10 for wasting human food. Another farmer in Yorkshire made up for shortage of cattle-cake by feeding his stock on bread: his exclamation, 'Well, I'll tell you straight, my cattle is going to have something', put a point of view deserving of sympathy, but he suffered three months' imprisonment.

From 'British Food Control', Sir William Beveridge.

In spite of the restrictions and apparent privation, one of the results of the First World War was an improvement in diet for the general population. The shocking condition of the majority of the young men called up for military service was recognised as being largely due to poor diet. As a result, there was a government drive to increase the welfare of young children with better school meals and physical training in the school curriculum. At the same time, the rise in wages during the war and immediate post-war years meant that the working classes suddenly had more money in their pockets than ever before, and much of this was spent on food. By 1920, wages had risen by more than 10 per cent in real terms while the eight hour working day was introduced. Other than among the war dead, life expectancy improved both through a significant decline in infant mortality and a general increase in longevity.

The Drink Question

The first decades of the Twentieth Century saw an ambivalent attitude towards alcohol. On the one hand, wine was regarded as having medicinal properties. Dr W. Lauzan-Brown, former sub-editor of the *Lancet*, in his *Useful Information for the Home* recommend burgundy for convalescence, anaemia, debility and loss of appetite; claret for 'powerful action for good' on the digestion and nervous system; port preventing colds and chills; sherry for exhaustion of the brain heart; and Champagne for ladies, convalescents and invalids. On the other hand, by early 1915 drink was regarded the authorities as a cause for concern. The war had broug in sexual promiscuity and widespread drunkenness. Lo Sandhurst was appalled. 'The effect of the war lower-class morals is amazing,' he declared. 'T whole country seems morally infected.' The too real possibility of dying young led ma to grasp whatever chance of fun there w available. It wasn't just the mc shipbuilders – a day late on urge repairs to a battleship through 'dri and conviviality' – who were in t

BETWEEN THE WARS

The twenties are often characterised as the Jazz Age or the 'Roaring Twenties', a period of wild abandon fuelled by a volatile cocktail of prohibition, rapid economic growth, the motor car and jazz. At least that was the case in the United States until it came to a shuddering halt with the Wall Street Crash in 1929. In Europe, unemployment and a struggle for economic survival curbed any general tendency towards hedonism, though there were a few notable exceptions, such as in Berlin under Weimar, or London, which had its fair share of flappers and cocktails. And while the hedonists may have been celebrated in fiction – Sally Bowles in Christopher Isherwood's *Farewell to Berlin* or the Great Gatsby in the novel of the same name by F. Scott Fitzgerald – most people

ublic houses supping ale and beer, it was the women war workers and
ousewives too. There were those in government who thought that
women should be banned from public houses, or even a general
rohibition brought in. Lloyd George made a resounding speech on the
ubject, saying, 'Drink is doing more damage in the War than all the
german submarines put together … We have got great powers to deal
with drink and we mean to use them.'

A press campaign against the demon drink began, and on Easter
Monday 1915 King George made 'The King's Pledge', vowing to support
he movement by 'giving up all alcoholic liquor himself, and issuing orders
against its consumption in the Royal Household, so that no difference shall
e made, so far as His Majesty is concerned, between the treatment of rich
nd poor in this question.' By the end of the year, a drink could only be
ought with a meal in hotels, restaurants and clubs. The purchase of spirits
was allowed only for half an hour on weekdays and increased duties made
he prices rise steeply. And public houses, which had formerly been open up
o 19 hours a day, were to be opened only from noon to 12.30 pm and from
.30 to 9.30 pm. These licensing laws were only marginally relaxed after
he war and remained substantially in place for decades.

barely dreamed of such frivolity, especially after the Great Depression began.

Changes were happening in food production, however, that were to affect
everyone. During the next two decades, food became increasingly
commercialised. Britain was the world's largest importer of tinned foods before
the first war had even started, and Heinz had already introduced baked beans
and were soon to open a factory in Harlesden. They were the tip of the iceberg
that embraced both labour-saving devices and convenience foods. The latter
included instant coffee, self-raising flour, custard powder and packet breakfast
cereals – the Shredded Wheat company opened a factory in Welwyn Garden
City. The new gas cookers, and later electric cookers, were some compensation
for the ever dwindling numbers of domestic servants. There were new gadgets

from the thirties onwards, everything from mincing machines to apple corers. And the domestic refrigerator was finally to liberate the housewife from the chore of shopping for fresh food daily. Now she could plan in advance, safe in the knowledge that the food would not spoil.

While convenience foods were produced by the new food entrepreneurs for use at home, there was also a new breed of catering entrepreneur, among whom in Britain the foremost was Jo Lyons. Though the first shop had been opened in Piccadilly Circus in 1894, it was not until the early Twentieth Century that the chain, known as Lyons Corner Houses, was to appear in cities all over the country. Milk bars – either independent outlets or part of a chain known as Black and White Milk Bars – offered cheap food in an alcohol-free environment. None of this, however, came anywhere near to approaching the concept of fine dining, though that did exist in clubs or in such restaurants as Quaglinos and Pruniers. Restaurant Boulestin opened in 1927 and boasted Britain's first broadcasting celebrity chef, Marcel Boulestin, who recorded a programme on

cookery for the BBC, as well as writing a cookery column in *Vogue* magazine.

The less well off city-dwellers, however, celebrated food rather differently – in the form of 'holidays' that exchanged one form of work for another. Many London families, for instance, would spend a week in Kent, picking fruit or, most popularly, hops. Hops were originally brought to the British Isles by the Romans who used the young shoots in salads, but in the Sixteenth Century hops began to be used in beer, helping to keep it drinkable for longer and giving it a new bitter flavour and aroma, different from the sweeter, often honey-flavoured ale. However, the hops all had to be picked at the same time in September and so working families would go down to the hop fields once a year, perhaps on the principle that a change was as good as a rest. It was certainly not a time to relax as George Orwell wrote in 1931:

> At about quarter past six in the morning we crawled out of straw, put on our coats and boots (we slept in everything else) and went out to get a fire going – rather a job this September, when it rained all the time. By half past six we had made tea and fried some bread for breakfast, and then we started off for work, with bacon sandwiches and a drum of cold tea for our dinner. If it didn't rain we were working pretty steadily till about one, and then we would start a fire between the vines, heat up our tea and knock off for half an hour. After that we were at it again till half past five, and by the time we had got home, cleaned the hop-juice off our hands and had tea, it was already dark and we were dropping with sleep. A good many nights, though, we used to go out and steal apples. There was a big orchard nearby, and three or four of us used to rob it systematically, carrying a sack and getting half a hundred-weight of apples at a time, besides several pounds of cobnuts. On Sunday we used to wash our shirts and socks in the stream, and sleep the rest of the day. As far as I can remember I never undressed completely all the time we were down there, nor washed my teeth, and only shaved twice a week. Between working and getting meals (and that meant fetching everlasting cans of water, struggling with wet faggots, frying in tin-lids etc) one seemed to have not an instant to spare.

From *The Collected Essays, Journalism and Letters of George Orwell*, 1968.

THE SECOND WORLD WAR

It is an irony – and one not lost on those who lived through it – that the diet of the general population during the Second World War in Britain was probably the healthiest that the Twentieth Century ever saw. Just as in the first war, though the food that Britain imported from the United States and Canada (around 55 million tons a year) was imperilled by German U-boats with the precise aim of destroying so many merchant ships that the country would be starved into submission. Around 2,500 cargo vessels were sunk and even Winston Churchill wrote: 'The only thing that ever really frightened me during the war was the U-boat peril.'

Not only was food not reaching the country, when it did come it was rationed, along with the food produced domestically. In fact, there had been plans about rationing as early as 1937. The underlying principle was a good one: that everyone, regardless of how rich or not they were, would be entitled to the same basic essential foodstuffs. And, while rationing levels would vary during the course of the war, at its height in 1942 a typical week's rations for each individual were:

> 115g / 4oz bacon and ham
> 1s 2d (around 6p) worth of meat – roughly, one pork chop and four sausages
> 55g / 2oz cheese (though sometimes it went up to 4 or even 8oz)
> 115g / 4oz margarine
> 55g / 2oz butter
> 1.7l / 3 pints milk (plus one packet of dried milk every month)
> 225g / 8oz sugar
> 1 egg
> 55g / 2oz tea

In addition, each individual would receive 450g / 1lb of jam every two months, 350g / 12oz of sweets a month and, for children (5–16), there was fruit and 300ml / ½ pint of milk a day, while younger children had extra orange juice and cod liver oil too.

At other times, oat flakes, canned tomatoes, biscuits, canned fruit, breakfast cereals and non-food essentials such as soap were rationed. Those living in the country or by the sea could supplement their diets with fish, game, rabbit and

The Great British Restaurant

During the Second World War, restaurants had a fixed price they could charge for a meal – five shillings (around 25p). However, there were also 'British Restaurants' run as non-profit making concerns by local Food Committees and they didn't require you to use up any of your valuable ration book coupons. The regulations stipulated that you could be served only one main course with either meat, game, poultry, fish, eggs or cheese. And the restaurants themselves were really more like canteens, rather bare, with long queues, but often very cheap. You could buy a meal for around one shilling and sixpence (around 8p).

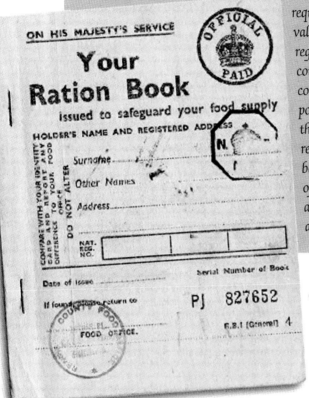

chicken, none of which were ever subject to rationing. But as supplies dwindled, other protein made its way onto the table, including horse and whale meat. Everyone, whether in town or country, was encouraged to 'Dig for Victory' and turn over their gardens to vegetables and fruits. The campaign covered not just private gardens, but included golf courses, parks, tennis court – even the moat of the Tower of London.

By 1943, over a million tons of vegetables were being grown in gardens and allotments. On the farms themselves, there was a severe shortage of labour. While the women's Land Army filled the roles vacated by the labourers who were now soldiers, at particular times of year there were still not enough hands to the plough. For seasonal work, such as planting potatoes in the spring and harvesting them in the autumn, this meant that children were issued with blue cards which allowed them to work a certain number of hours of the school term out in the fields, 'tattie-picking'.

For those in the cities, though, there was less opportunity to fish, catch game or grow as many vegetables, and supplies in the shops were low enough in the summer of 1941 to prompt the greengrocers to leave the towns in search of fresh vegetables from the country. This was a short-lived solution as petrol rationing was soon to come into force.

The entire country, however, had to come up with some ingenious ideas for eking out their meagre rations and maintaining a healthy diet. So, if you could find a decent piece of meat by combining your family's rations together, you would cook it as a real Sunday treat, make the remains into a stew for Monday and the remains of that into Bubble and Squeak on Tuesday. Tea leaves were reused, cakes were made with dried egg (so the real egg could be saved for more important use), bread and dripping was a teatime favourite, unusual animal parts (pigs' feet and ears, soup made with fish heads) were employed and, all in all, the nation made do. As a result, they were all far healthier. In spite of the bread and dripping, they ate less fat and, of course, meat but lots more vegetables. The daily calorie intake fell from 3,000 to 2,800, and they were far more active than we are today.

THE COMMERCIALISATION OF FOOD

Rationing finally disappeared in Britain in the early 1950s and there was great excitement each time a food – such as bananas – reappeared after its absence during the war years. Unfortunately, at the same time, the culinary arts were at an all-time low. Perhaps it was because people were used to struggling with the most limited ingredients, perhaps women preferred being in full-time employment to being the angel in the family home, perhaps everyone had simply forgotten how to cook or, growing up during the war, had never learned. There were, nevertheless, great steps forward in food technology, the most significant of which was freezing. Frozen fruit and vegetables appeared in the shops, though they were eaten as soon as they defrosted as home freezers did not appear in any numbers until the 1970s. The same decade saw the introduction of the microwave oven.

The void left by the lack of honed cooking skills was soon filled by the

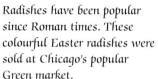

Seasonal fruit is flown in from all over the world with an emphasis on regularity of shape, this is now being revised in light of concern for carbon footprints.

Radishes have been popular since Roman times. These colourful Easter radishes were sold at Chicago's popular Green market.

Exotic fruits are now taken for granted. When the banana was first seen in England after the Second World War, many people didn't realise they had to peel it first. For many people, the pineapple can be too complicated to peel – or was turned into the infamous pineapple hedgehog in the 1970s.

noisome American invention of fast food. It began in the 1950s with the Wimpy Bar, continued in the 1960s with Kentucky Fried Chicken and McDonald's in the 1970s. In the meantime, the post-war collapse of the British Empire led to the boom in ethnic restaurants, particularly Chinese and Indian, and the appearance in the shops and food markets of such exotic Caribbean foods as yams, mangoes and plantains – never been seen before in Britain.

From the 1980s onwards, celebrity chefs were only a part of the backlash against processed and fast foods, globalisation and the loss of local character in cooking. As the British began to travel abroad more widely and frequently, there was an increasing admiration for how other cultures approached food. The 'foodie' was born, touring Europe and beyond to savour French cheeses and

Naff Food, Nouvelle Food

The 1960s and 1970s were a period of great change and social mobility. New foods, eating out in restaurants and entertaining at home all became popular, but there was little experience of either fine dining or cooking. Many foods had not been seen in Britain for years and no one really knew what to do with them. So there was no help at home, and, while there was more disposable income, there was little travel – for many years there were stringent limits on the amount of money that could be taken out of the UK. Even our European neighbours were not within reach for advice on how to prepare and present our food. Our resulting attempts were often comic. Cocktail sticks adorned with a cube of cheese and a piece of pineapple – or even grouped pineapple cocktail sticks to form a pineapple 'hedgehog' – became favourite party pieces. Prawn cocktails and Black Forest gateaux became almost the only choice of first and final courses in many restaurants. Stuffed mushrooms were thought to be the height of elegance – their demise only came when Shirley Conran announced 'Life's too short to stuff a mushroom.' To be fair, there were not too many good ingredients to choose from. Ham was a limp watery affair, a million miles from Parma or Bayonne. Tuna came out of a can. In many supermarkets, cheese was often a choice of Cheddar or cottage. Bread was like cardboard.

Italian hams, Greek olive oils, Spanish chorizo and Moroccan couscous. There was a realisation that Britain's own local cheeses and rare breeds of farm animals could be lost forever. Campaigns for 'real' food began – the great grandaddy of them all being CAMRA (the Campaign for Real Ale), which was founded back in the 1970s with the aim of stopping the spread of the homogeneous beer being sold by the big breweries and ensuring the survival of local ales that had been associated with their regions, sometimes for centuries.

CAMRA was the first great success but many have followed. Bottled mineral water was scoffed at in Britain until it became a regular feature on supermarket shelves and in restaurants. The rise of organic farming has been meteoric despite generally higher prices. As famous chefs began to stipulate to

A further change was, however, at hand. The late 1970s and 1980s saw the rise of nouvelle cuisine. While Britain – and most especially London – had seen a number of improvements on the restaurant scene, this movement, which began in France rather earlier, transformed how food was presented in this country. Far smaller portions were beautifully arranged on plates, innovative ingredients appeared, some of which, like the kiwi fruit, eventually became a cliché in their own right. Food was as fresh as possible and cooked more lightly and without rich sauces. Because of its lack of butter, cream and other fattening ingredients, it was also known as 'cuisine minceur' – slimming cookery. By the mid 1980s it had reached its peak and began to decline into a caricature of itself, but its influence in the long-term was beneficial, and was the start of the interest in and clamour for 'real food'.

It was the beginning of globalisation – that process by which an overwhelming choice of food could be brought to the wealthy developed world so that we could enjoy whatever we wanted, whatever the season. At the same time, though, the choice of places to which that food could be bought dwindled as supermarket chains increased in size and marketing strength. And, with the growth of the supermarkets came the growth, too, of processed foods – prepared, chilled or frozen and ready simply to pop into the microwave. Not only did people feel they no longer needed to learn how to cook, they lost all connection with where their food came from.

It seems strange then that this has been the era of the celebrity chef. The first celebrity chef was probably Antonin Carême, 'the chef of kings and the king of chefs', but the concept is really a late Twentieth Century one, and one that is directly related to television. From Delia Smith to Marco Pierre White and from Jamie Oliver to Nigella Lawson, each has his or her own unique selling point – be that sex appeal or an appalling temper. They make fortunes from television series and their books sell like hot cakes, but for a vast number of people, that is as far as their interest stretches. They don't actually get into the kitchen and start cooking as the ever-rising sales of ready meals attest.

Traditional markets, such as this one, are now vying with farmers' markets as more people want locally-grown produce which follows the seasons.

their suppliers that they knew the provenance of animals – partly a reaction to outbreaks of disease and partly due to the improved taste of rare breeds of farm animals or those raised in particular conditions – 'sourcing' became important. High-class butchers could tell their customers where their Welsh black beef or lamb raised on salt marshes came from, down to the farm or even the individual animal. Farmers' markets flourished selling free range, organic, fresh produce all over the country. This idea became particularly popular after the awareness of 'food miles' – the vast distances food had to travel to the supermarket shelf, and the impact this would have on climate change – began to grow.

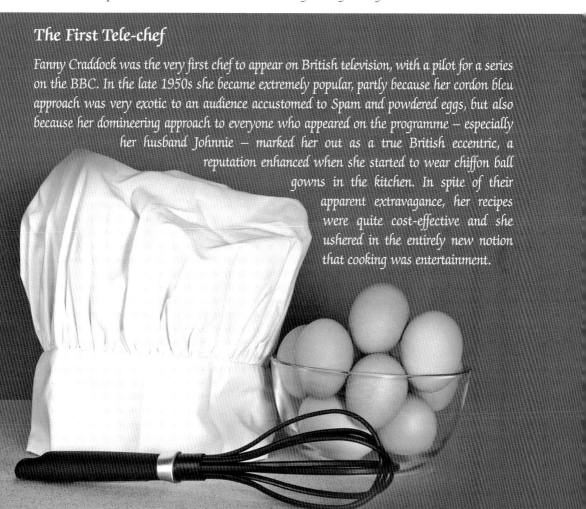

The First Tele-chef

Fanny Craddock was the very first chef to appear on British television, with a pilot for a series on the BBC. In the late 1950s she became extremely popular, partly because her cordon bleu approach was very exotic to an audience accustomed to Spam and powdered eggs, but also because her domineering approach to everyone who appeared on the programme – especially her husband Johnnie – marked her out as a true British eccentric, a reputation enhanced when she started to wear chiffon ball gowns in the kitchen. In spite of their apparent extravagance, her recipes were quite cost-effective and she ushered in the entirely new notion that cooking was entertainment.

Obesity, though, is still an epidemic and the burger bars still have plenty of customers, but after decades of cheap, fast food that has travelled many miles to reach us, it would seem that at the beginning of the Twenty-first Century, a significant minority of people are making changes to their diets. As weight problems, heart disease and cancers are increasingly related to diet and lifestyle, the idea of slow cooking and 'real' food seems to be more and more in vogue. The threat of global warming makes local, seasonal, organic food ever more appealing. The importance of healthy eating is stressed in magazines, books and newspapers, on television and in government campaigns. Cooking from healthy, raw ingredients is regarded as better than ready meals and food is even seen as having medicinal properties. It all sounds eerily familiar – would the Medieval monk in his walled garden, Nicholas Culpeper writing his herbal, or even Mrs Beeton have any quarrel with such an idea? Probably not. At the beginning of a new millennium, it looks as if our approach to food may just be turning full circle.

TWENTIETH CENTURY COOKBOOK

The Twentieth Century has seen so many changes in our approach to food, this final cookbook section gives just a few examples of some of those from its earlier years.

Edwardian Violet Salad

This Edwardian salad is from *Meals Medicinal* by Dr W. T. Fernie (1905) and, suitable for delicate invalids, reflects the last era when the kitchen, rather than medicine provided convalescence:

Take a Batavian endive, some finely curled celery, a sprinkle of minced parsley, a single olive, and the petals of a couple of dozen blue violets. These several ingredients are to be mixed with the purest olive oil, salt and pepper being the only condiment. Add a dash of Bordeaux wine and a suspicion of white vinegar.

Rizzared Haddie

S. Beaty-Pownall 1901 wrote *Breakfast and Lunch Dishes* in 1901 and this recipe no doubt featured on the breakfast menu of Edwardian shooting parties in the highlands:

A very popular Scots breakfast dish. For this rub the fish well, inside and out, with salt and after running a skewer through their heads fasten them up in the open air supporting the ends of the skewer on two trivets, and leave them there for 24 hours. Then skin them, dust them with flour and grill over a clear fire. Many fish can be cooked in this way, plaice and flounders being particularly good, but cut off the heads and let them hang head down to drain for 24 hours before use as this makes them finer and less watery.

Mock Steak

This recipe appeared in *Camp Cookery* published by the Ceylon Army Command shortly before the Second World War:

A good method of using up the stewing portions of the beef ration or local beef is as follows:

4^{1}/$_{2kg}$ / 10lb beef
900g / 2lb 4oz onions
Pepper and salt, to taste

Pass raw beef and onion through mincer, add pepper and salt as required, then mix well by hand and place in baking dishes not exceeding ^{1}/$_{2}$ inch thickness. Proceed to press down the ingredients firmly with the palm of the hand. This will ensure that the mixture when cooked is set in one portion. Then cover the whole with stock or water and bake in a hot oven for a period of 1^{1}/$_{4}$ hours. Serve in squares with onion sauce.

Green Pineapples

Another recipe from *Camp Cookery*, this one sent in by Gunner Johns, proving how the British Tommie coped with the local food:

> Skin the fruit. Cut into pieces. Put into a clean pan, adding water just to cover, and bring to the boil. Let it simmer for 1 hour, add a little milk, then beat up an egg in sugar, add this and let it simmer for 5 minutes. Cool and serve.

Spam Fritters

This must be the ultimate wartime recipe

1 tin of spam
2 tbsp dried egg powder
$1^1/4$ tbsp flour
Knob of lard
Milk and water mixed

Cut the spam into four slices. Mix together the flour and egg, gradually adding the mixed milk and water until you have a thin batter. Melt the lard in a frying pan, dip each slice of spam in the batter to coat and fry.

Glossary

Chirugery	– Surgery
Cury	– Medieval term for cookery
Custarde/crustarde	– A Medieval open pie of cream, eggs and dates
Frumenty	– Medieval cereal-based soup
Hippocras	– A sweet wine, very expensive
Liquamen	– Salty fish sauce used by Romans
Mortrew	– Medieval meaty soup
Payne Puff	– A Medieval sweet dish with egg yolks, bone marrow, dates, raisins and ginger
Pippins	– Small apples
Pottage	– Medieval and Tudor soup
Powder douce	– Mixed sweet spices
Receipt	– Recipe
Sallett	– A salad or dish made from cooked vegetables
Soteltee	– A food sculpture used as a table centrepiece from Medieval times
Thermopolia	– Roman food shops
Trencher	– A large piece of stale bread used as a plate
Verjuice	– Sour grape juice

Acknowledgements

Thanks to Carlotta Barrow who lent me armfuls of books, including *Camp Cookery*, which had been illustrated by her father. Thanks also to Hilda Richardson (aka my mum) who recalled wartime privations and the recipe for spam fritters.

Margaret Visser's masterly *The Rituals of Dinner* was full of valuable observations on our changing manners and what they signify.

Daniel Myers was very helpful in Medieval and Tudor recipes and all matters relating to them. Translater Christanne Muusers deserves thanks, too. Daniel Myers' website www.medievalcookery.com is an excellent source of updated versions of original recipes. Thanks also to the Carnegie Mellons School of Computer Science that has some fascinating Roman recipes on its website, which proved to be very useful, www.cs.cmu.edu/~mjw/recipes/ethnic/historical/ant-rom-coll.html

The British Library has a vast resource of cookery books throughout all periods of history from Medieval manuscripts up to the present day and I am most grateful for those they have supplied for this book.

Permissions

The author would like to thank the following for their help in providing images:

Cheffins Auctioneers – 143, 148 (bottom)

Derrick Hemingway – 43

Donna M Hemingway – 32

Simon Ho, www.simonho.org - 107

Lawrences Fine Art Auctioneers of Crewkerne – 106, 127, 148 (top)

The Royal Pavilion, Libraries & Museums, Brighton & Hove – Cover
    illustration, 130, 131, 134

Ruthin Castle Medieval banquets – 66

Fiona Shoop – 10, 22, 31, 33, 42 (bottom), 44, 53, 98, 118, 149, 165, 168

The Watercress Alliance, www.watercress.co.uk/ – 153

With thanks to Shutterstock for the remainder of the images

Bibliography

Acton, Eliza, *Modern Cookery for Private Families*, 1845

Beckett, Ian F. W., *The Great War*, Longman, 2001

Braudel, Fernand, *The Structures of Everyday Life*, William Collins, 1981

Craig, Diana, *Cooks' Wisdom*, Inklink, 1992

Culpeper, Nicholas, *Culpeper's Compleat Herbal*, c.1640

Davies, Norman, *Europe, a History*, Oxford University Press, 1966

Dickens, Charles, *The Old Curiosity Shop*, 1841

Faas, Patrick, *Around the Roman Table – Food and Feasting in Ancient Rome*, University of Chicago Press, 2003

Fraser, Flora, *The English Gentlewoman*, Barrie & Jenkins, 1987

Girouard, Mark, *A Country House Companion*, Century Hutchinson, 1987

Gough, Richard, *The History of Myddle*, c. 1706

Hibbert, Christopher, *The English, a Social History*, William Collins, 1987

Hutchins, Sheila, *English Recipes*, Methuen, 1967

Mabey, David, *In Search of Food*, Macdonald & Janes, 1978

Priestley, J. B., *English Humour*, Heinemann, 1976

Visser, Margaret, *The Rituals of Dinner*, Viking, 1992

Williams, John, *The Home Fronts 1914–1918*, Constable, 1972

Wilson, Trevor, *The Myriad Faces of War*, Polity Press, 1986

Sources

http://www.harvestfields.ca/CookBooks/003/07/00.htm

http://www.coquinaria.nl/kooktekst/Edelikespijse0.htm

http://www.hti.umich.edu/cgi/t/text/text-idx?c=cme;idno=CookBk

http://staff-www.uni-marburg.de/%7Egloning/ouv3.htm

http://www.medievalcookery.com/notes/ouverture.shtm

http://www.medievalcookery.com/books.html#TFCCB

http://www.medievalcookery.com/recipes/douce.shtm

http://www.daviddfriedman.com/Medieval/Cookbooks/Menagier/Menagier.html

http://www.uni-giessen.de/gloning/tx/1615murr.htm
http://www.medievalcookery.com/books.html#GHJ
http://www.medievalcookery.com/books.html#PNBOC
http://staff-www.uni-marburg.de/~gloning/1615murr.htm
http://www.medievalcookery.com/books.html#PNBOC
http://www.medievalcookery.com/notes/ouverture.shtm

Index